Mentoring
in action

**A PRACTICAL
GUIDE
FOR MANAGERS**

DAVID MEGGINSON &

DAVID CLUTTERBUCK

Mentoring
in action

A PRACTICAL
GUIDE
FOR MANAGERS

KOGAN
PAGE

YOURS TO HAVE AND TO HOLD

BUT NOT TO COPY

First published in 1995

Kogan Page Limited
120 Pentonville Road
London N1 9JN

© David Megginson and David Clutterbuck, 1995

British Library Cataloguing in Publication Data

A CIP record for this book is available from the British Library.

ISBN 0 7494 1390 5

Typeset by Kogan Page
Printed in England by Clays Ltd, St Ives plc

Contents

Chapter 3: Individual Cases   167

LIST OF CONTRIBUTORS

Mike Allen is the head of IS branch at the headquarters of the British government's Employment Department. He is also chair of the Advisory Board of Sheffield Hallam University's MSc IT and Management.

Liz Borredon has worked at the Counselling and Career Development Unit of Leeds University, and has co-founded a residential centre for management training. She moved to France in 1990 to teach at EDHEC Graduate Business School, Lille. She is the French link-person of the European Mentoring Centre.

David Clutterbuck has written or co-authored more than 20 management books, including the best-selling *The Winning Streak*. In recent years, he has focused on quality themes, becoming the recognized European expert on service quality strategies and carrying out a variety of research projects to identify best practice in empowerment. He also acts as a consultant to major UK and international companies.

Chairman of The ITEM Group plc, senior partner of business research consultancy Clutterbuck Associates and director of The European Mentoring Centre, David Clutterbuck holds academic posts at Putteridge Bury and Sheffield Business Schools, in addition to the International Management Centres. He was founder editor of the management journals *Issues, Marketing Business* and *Strategic Direction;* he also launched Tom Peters' newsletter, *On Achieving Excellence*, in Europe.

Mary Evans works as a management development consultant within Lewisham Council providing professional leadership, consultancy and support to all those – managers, HR professionals and trainers – responsible for developing managers in the organization. In addition, she has particular responsibility for the corporate initiatives designed to aid the internal career development of women and black staff, and runs the Council's Sponsor Scheme – a mentoring programme for black staff.

Pam Fricker is a team leader in Benefits Agency Training Operations, responsible for providing a training and consultancy service to approximately 3000 Benefits Agency staff in the South East area. Pam's involvement in mentoring began in 1993, when the area launched a development scheme, and Pam was asked to design, and deliver, training for the participants in the scheme and their mentors. Since then she has also been involved in training mentors in other, more local, programmes.

Coral Gardiner is the Mentoring Development Officer for the West Midlands Probation Service. Ms Gardiner's involvement in mentoring includes the establishment of the Birmingham wide BEAT Project which is supported by WMPS, Birmingham TEC, Careers Service and the Birmingham City Council. She works as the Consultant/Trainer in all aspects of mentoring structure, systems and development for the West Midlands County Probation Service.

Bob Garvey is a lecturer in Performance Management at Durham University Business School. His interest in mentoring stems from work over many years in a range of organizations striving to achieve effective organizational learning. He is currently researching a Health Service mentor scheme, and providing consultancy on mentoring in a range of organizations in the North East of Britain.

Michael Green is managing partner in Transitional Space, a consultancy specializing in aiding individuals and teams to develop themselves and their organizations. He has a background in human resource management, management and organizational development. He is also a UK registered psychotherapist and his approach within organizations is informed by both the analytic and integrative schools of psychotherapy. Michael has been involved in several projects that have used external mentoring as an integral part of the organization's development. These have ranged from full blown corporate transformation projects, through top team mentoring, to tackling individual behavioural and performance issues. He has written papers on individual and top team mentoring and mentoring for organizational change.

Linda Holbeche is assistant director of Roffey Park Management College, following a career in industry that culminated in her becoming Management Development Manager for a large financial services company.

Jöran Hultman has been a consultant in the development of leadership and mentoring since 1992. He was formerly personnel director for Svenska Nestlé AB in Sweden. He introduced mentoring in his company in 1982 and is also the author of the book *The Mentor – a practical guide*.

Lesley Martinson worked as a trainer and training manager for the Department of Environment. She is currently a development advisor in the Cabinet Office, Office of Public Service, Development Division, offering guidance to human resource practitioners in Civil Service organizations on setting up mentoring schemes.

Norman McLean is Director of the Mentor Unit of the National Mentoring Consortium at the University of East London.

David Megginson is a writer and researcher on self-development and the line manager as developer. He has written *A Manager's Guide to Coaching*, *Self-development: a Facilitator's Guide*, and *Human resource Development* in Kogan Page's Fast-track MBA series, *The Line Manager as Developer* and the *Developing the Developers* research report. He consults and researches in blue chip companies, with top teams of small companies and public and voluntary organizations. He is a Director of the European Mentoring Centre and of Mentoring Directors Ltd. He is an elected council member of the association for Management Education and Development, and has been associate head of Sheffield Business School and a national assessor for the National Training Awards.

Julie White was a post-graduate student at Sheffield Business School with a special interest in understanding the sources of energy for development in organizations.

PART 1
The State of the Art

1
MENTORING IN ACTION

INTRODUCTION

In this book you will find an introduction to the state of the art of mentoring as revealed by the literature and by our experiences of working with mentors, learners and mentoring schemes. There then follows a series of case studies of contrasting schemes, and a number of stories of individual mentoring relationships. Because mentoring is such a private relationship it is unusual to get this kind of insight into what goes on face to face, so these one-to-one accounts offer many new insights. Finally, all this material is drawn together to build a picture of mentoring in the future, which will act as a guide for learners, mentors and scheme organizers.

In this chapter we examine the state of mentoring and notice how it is flourishing in a hundred guises. We examine why this is so. What are the conditions in organizations, individuals and careers that make mentoring so popular? We ask what mentoring is, and aim to discover the irreducible core of experiences that is labelled mentoring.

WHAT IS MENTORING?

Our preferred definition of mentoring is that it is:

> off-line help by one person to another in making significant transitions in knowledge, work or thinking.

There is a lot in these few words, so we will highlight some of the features of our definition that point up the particular nature of the mentoring process.

First we see mentoring as off-line; that is it is not normally the job of a line manager. A mentor is usually more senior or experienced than the learner, but there are also cases of peer mentoring that work very successfully. On occasion in formal schemes and more often in natural, spontaneous or informal mentoring relationships, the mentor is also the line manager. Where we find line managers successfully acting as mentors, they seem to have a highly developed capacity to separate out the two functions. The line responsibility is often about pressure for immediate results. The mentoring relationship tends more towards giving time and space for taking a wider view. Skilled mentors make these distinctions clear, even if they do not always formally say: 'This is now a mentoring session'. The message becomes clear as the meeting progresses.

Something that makes mentoring exchanges different, whatever role the mentor has, is also captured in our definition: mentoring is about support in significant transitions. There is a Latin tag about the law not being concerned with trivia, and the same could be said for mentoring. Put another way, the mentor has a role to help the learner grasp the wider significance of whatever is happening, where at first it might appear trifling or insignificant.

A final feature of our definition is that mentoring is about one person helping one other. There is an example in this book of a scheme, described by Michael Green, which uses group mentors. We leave it to our readers to decide whether this falls within the boundary of what they consider mentoring to be. The case is useful, because it is on the edge of the field and challenges us to consider our view on this matter.

THE STATE OF THE ART

At the 1994 European Mentoring Centre/Sheffield Business School Mentoring Research Conference (Megginson, Clutterbuck and Whitaker, 1994) we noted that it was clear that the field of mentoring is both well established and wide open for growth and innovation in the areas of practice and theory. The power of mentoring to change mind-sets was seen as well established. This confirmed the research that had been carried out in the previous few years that mentoring had been increasing in significance for developers and for people seeking development.

The *Developing the Developers* research (Boydell et al., 1991) asked 633 developers which developmental approaches of over 80 they intended to use in the future. Mentoring was chosen more frequently than all the other methods except for team building. Coaching was placed third. This was confirmed by an Industrial Society (1992) survey the next year, which also placed mentoring above coaching.

Research that has been carried out in the UK has indicated that the British approach to mentoring differs from that in the USA. In an article by Gibb and Megginson (1993) we reported that in America mentoring focused upon career and psychosocial functions. In Britain, by contrast, learning was becoming more important as a focus, and, for some, the emphasis on the mentor sponsoring someone's career was seen as not legitimate.

These findings are summarized below. The American agenda addressed the following issues that enhanced career advancement:

☐ *sponsorship* – for career advancement

☐ *exposure and visibility* – bringing the learner to others' attention

☐ *coaching* – helping performance on the job

☐ *protection* – the opposite side of the coin from sponsorship

☐ *challenging assignments*.

The American research also showed that there was a strong psychosocial element in mentoring there, including:

☐ *role modelling* – demonstrating how to handle themselves in the organization or the role

☐ *acceptance and confirmation* – personal support

☐ *counselling* – dealing with personal issues which may or may not relate directly to work

☐ *friendship* – building on the personal dimension of the relationship.

The British experience, which is reinforced by the studies in this book, was somewhat different. Although some of the features of American mentoring were present, there was also a different agenda. The four roles we identified were:

☐ improve performance

☐ career development

☐ counsellor

☐ sharing knowledge.

Each of these roles had a British slant on it which differentiated it from the American experience. Improving performance, which relates to the 'coaching' in the American list, was either the most important or the least important of the roles in the British schemes surveyed. This suggests that a polarization was taking place – some schemes are about the current job and improving performance, others take a wider, career and learning-focused view. It could be argued that schemes focusing solely upon performance improvement are not really mentoring at all, but our experience was that the schemes in Britain did not do this, and even those that put performance first also addressed the rest of the British agenda. So, mentoring is multi-faceted.

Career development in Britain is not a matter of sponsorship giving a disproportionate advantage to the learner over their peers who were not being mentored. It is more about giving the learner an opportunity to think through their career direction and to make choices and pursue options on their own behalf. In Britain, there seems to be a caution about mentoring favouring the learner too much, and steps are taken to prevent this happening, or alternatively of allowing everyone to have the opportunity to have a mentor. Sponsorship is, however, widely seen to be justified when the mentoring is designed to compensate for disadvantage in employment caused by race, gender, age or a record of offending. There are a number of heartening examples in this book of the mentor unashamedly sponsoring such disadvantaged individuals to good effect in a way that it would be churlish to take exception to.

The counselling role tends in Britain to focus more upon work issues than upon personal aspects of the life of the learner. Clearly, as a relationship deepens the two tend to become harder to separate. However, the greater social distance between people in Britain, and the reticence about entering into counselling relationships, means that this role is more circumscribed in Britain than in America.

Finally, sharing knowledge was a growing issue in mentoring relationships in Britain, whereas it did not appear on the agenda in the studies of American mentoring that had been undertaken ten years earlier. In the British schemes, sharing knowledge was virtually never the main role of the mentor but it was often the second most important one of the four. This seems to have come about because many mentoring schemes in Britain have grown out of support for learners attending a part-time course of study.

The EMC/SBS conference referred to earlier also served to remind us that there was a need to *reinstate the learner* at the top of the agenda. In recent years, with the development of new applications of mentoring and schemes for delivering them, structural issues have been foremost in the concerns of both practitioners and researchers. When individuals *have* been considered, the emphasis has been on the mentors. The need to consider their selection and training has been paramount. However, at the conference, we recognised the importance, for both theorists and practitioners, of *shifting the focus onto the learner*.

The centrality of the learner in the relationship is confirmed by some research carried out in Motorola by Richard Caruso (1992). He concluded that, in the well-established scheme in Motorola, mentoring was seen as a dispersed, mentee-driven activity. By this he meant that mentees, in practice, made choices of who they would seek help from, and typically selected from a range of choices, which might include several mentors. This finding has been confirmed in research by Caroline Altounyan (1995), who has examined the sources of support taken up by part-time personnel management students. She found that students used formal and self-chosen informal mentors as well as their line managers, tutors and other students on the course.

Measuring the effects of mentoring

Recent work with a number of organizations by the European Mentoring Centre indicates that there are a few basic elements to measuring mentoring, as shown below:

Programme level		
Relationship level		

           Process   Outputs

Relatively few schemes carry out systematic evaluation, but we believe this is an important part of maintaining the credibility of mentoring and relating it to business benefit.

Measuring *relationship processes* asks questions such as:

□   have mentor and mentee established a close rapport?

□   does the relationship have a clear objective, committed to by both parties?

□   are meetings sufficiently frequent?

□   are they sufficiently to the point?

□   are they valued by mentor and mentee?

□   are both mentor and mentee learning?

Measuring *relationship outputs* focuses on more quantitative data. For example, hard measures might be:

□   how many of our learning milestones did we reach?

□   has the mentee improved key scores on his or her performance appraisal?

Soft measures could be:

□   does the mentee feel more confident in his or her ability to tackle new challenges?

□   does the line manager feel that mentoring is helping the mentee make progress?

Clearly, the ability to achieve quantifiable measurements at the relationship level will depend to a considerable extent upon the clarity of the objectives of the programme.

Measuring *programme processes* may be a matter of simply aggregating the experiences of mentoring pairs. But it may also involve questions such as:

☐ were the selection criteria adequate?

☐ what proportion of relationships succeeded and failed?

☐ do mentors feel they had sufficient training?

☐ what skills deficiencies do mentees perceive in their mentors?

☐ is the programme support sufficient?

Measuring *programme outputs*. Again, these might be *hard*, eg:

☐ decrease in turnover of graduates/junior managers

☐ achievement of improved appraisal scores on key competencies

☐ number of mentees considered suitable for promotion after a set period.

Or *soft*, eg:

☐ proportion of mentors/mentees who believe they have achieved significant progress through the relationship

☐ perception of mentor's direct reports on the improvement in his or her dealings with them.

APPLICATIONS AREAS

Mentoring is spreading rapidly outside the business areas too. A remarkable diversity of schemes can be seen in schools and universities, among fledgeling entrepreneurs, disadvantaged minorities and even among recently released prisoners. Mentoring is so flexible an approach that it can help almost any group of people with difficult transitions to make.

In business and the public sector, there are mentoring schemes for:

☐ *Graduate recruits.* The most common form of business mentoring, graduate induction's popularity stems from its efficacy in attracting and keeping a valuable human resource.

☐ *Junior managers and supervisors,* especially where these have missed out on formal training.

☐ *People moving into head office from the field.* To help people withstand the culture shock of moving to Somerset House, the Inland Revenue provides 'old hands' or mentors, who can reassure the newcomer that the stresses and strains will diminish.

☐ *Disadvantaged groups,* such as women who have reached the glass ceiling. Volvo and Ireland's Aer Rianta are among companies with this kind of scheme.

☐ *Local citizens in developing countries,* where the government is keen to promote its citizens into jobs currently held by ex-patriates.

☐ *Newly qualified professionals,* such as members of the Institute of Personnel and Development (IPD) who may receive as mentor someone who is highly experienced from another company.

☐ *People about to take up major job challenges,* for example, Store Managers (designate) at Asda.

☐ *Top management.* An increasing proportion of CEOs and directors are seeking help from mentors. These tend to be people outside the organisation, for obvious reasons.

In education, mentors are frequently assigned to:

☐ *Student teachers,* especially in their final year of tuition and first year after graduation.

☐ *University students 'at risk' and disadvantaged schoolchildren.* Students from disadvantaged backgrounds have a higher dropout rate that can be countered by effective mentoring.

☐ *Gifted schoolchildren* schemes in the USA match retired engineers, musicians and other people with expertise with youngsters who have similar talent. The relationship encourages the child to persist with its studies and practise.

☐ *New head teachers* in many areas of the country are entitled to a mentor for the first year or two of their new job.

☐ *New lecturers* in universities. At Sheffield Hallam University all new lecturers are offered a mentor, an experienced lecturer who has volunteered to share their experience and has been trained to do so.

In the community, mentoring schemes are used to:

☐ *Help mentally and physically handicapped people into employment*, for example, the Rathbone Trust.

☐ *Keep young people on probation out of trouble* (see the BEAT scheme, pages 44-57).

☐ *Support people starting small businesses*, by linking them with a big company mentor. The entrepreneurs not only get the benefit of the mentor's experience, but access to free, in-depth guidance from the mentor's colleagues.

Why business is taking to mentoring

A number of trends have combined to raise the profile of mentoring in business. Among them is *the changing role of training and development*. The question 'How do we add value?' has increasing importance for the training and development (T&D) function. Frequently whittled down to a half or less of its size a decade ago, T&D is expected to do more with less. Inevitably, that reinforces the requirement to push responsibility for developing talent and career management on to the line and to the individual employee. T&D's role becomes increasingly one of co-ordination, resourcing and helping line managers develop others.

Mentoring meets a strong current need because line managers frequently have great difficulty coping with broader development issues. Coaching people to improve their skill at current tasks is relatively easy, if the manager is prepared to put aside the required quality time. But development often requires a different perspective – an ability to put aside the current task and examine future possibilities. At its best, it also requires a relationship of trust which is very difficult to achieve in a judgemental relationship – yet line managers are under pressure to be judgemental, both to maintain discipline and to carry out performance appraisals, with their inherent undertones of punishment and reward. The mentor, as an off-line friend with no such impediments, provides an ideal second opinion.

T&D is also under considerable pressure to show results. Because well-constructed mentoring programmes automatically set quantifiable objectives, they help T&D demonstrate its contribution to the business. It is no coincidence that the programme objectives for many mentoring projects echo the language of the company's key corporate objectives.

Mentoring is also attractive to T&D because it requires a relatively low input from the T&D budget for mentor and learner training, and for programme administration. Most of the cost is borne by the line, in terms of the time spent by mentor and learner. There is also a pay-off for T&D in the fact that mentoring provides a two-for-one benefit – so much so that in some organizations mentoring has been sold to top management primarily on the basis of the learning for *mentors*.

WHY MENTORING NOW?

There seem to us to be a number of factors that converge to make mentoring a method of the times. The ones that stand out are:

□   the reduction in the capacity of personnel and training departments

□   pressures on the role of the line manager

□   the move towards learning companies

□   new perspectives on careers

□   changing professional requirements.

The capacity of training departments

The reduction in the size of personnel and training departments (for example, recently British Telecom announced a halving of its personnel department) means that they have less *internal* resource to provide for the direct development of individuals. In many organizations they also have less budget for running internal events or for sending people off on expensive external courses. The pressure on time seems to continue to increase. In the past 30 years, courses have shrunk from a fortnight to a week, to a couple of days, to a day or even less in many organizations today. There is also a sharper demand from power-holders in organizations for an increase in the relevance and immediacy of application of learning. Additionally, there is a widespread demand from people in organizations that learning be related to the organization's strategy.

The combined effect of all these factors is that the human resource management/development departments are less significant players in the direct provision of learning opportunities.

Pressure on the contribution of the line manager

This raises the question of who is to fill the role that was previously held by the full-time T&D people. In many organizations greater pressure is being put upon line managers to develop their own staff. They are asked to move towards the role of teacher, educator, developer or coach. The advantages of this proposed solution are that the cost of line managers doing these activities is effectively hidden, as they do it in the time that they would have been working for the organization anyway, so there are no identifiable costs associated with this work. There are opportunity costs, in terms of their being unable to do other things while they are developing their staff. People who are keen on this solution say that even these opportunity costs are negligible, as acting as a developer of your people saves time that would otherwise be spent on controlling staff or correcting the errors and answering the queries of staff who were less able to function effectively in a relatively autonomous role.

However, many organizations are finding that line managers are overburdened. The increasing rate of stress and excessive hours among managers is well documented. There is ample evidence that the formal requirement on managers to develop their staff, such as the carrying out of staff appraisal or development review, is often not done at all or only done with extreme reluctance, under pressure and late. It is our experience that this does not arise so much from incompetence or unwillingness on the part of line managers as from an unbearable pressure of other demands on their time. Delayering has led to an increase in the number of direct reports that they have. Other systems of support that would be needed to enable them to discharge their developmental duties have not been put in place. In particular, management information systems that are user friendly and available to managers and all their staff are the exception rather than the rule in today's organizations. This defect is particularly marked in the public sector, but the lack of information systems is also widespread in private sector organizations.

All this means that line managers are often unable to carry out the developer's role to the full. Additionally, in many organizations, the role of the line manager has a heavy requirement for control. Middle managers are appointed to make sure that the ship is kept tight and there is no leakage of resources through inefficiency, slackness or fraud. Whatever the wishes of individual managers in these circumstances, there will be strong pressures for development to be set on one side.

Finally, in many organizations, with project-based management or matrix structures, it is becoming increasingly hard to work out who is anyone's line manager anyway! Multiple bosses or diffused leadership roles are often pointed to as a weakness of matrix-type organizations. However, it is worth pointing out that proponents of this form have, from the early 1970s, insisted that it is only viable in an organization culture where there is a high level of interpersonal skill. Staff need to be able to manage upwards and to negotiate a constructive accommodation of the conflicting demands for their time and attention. There are suggestions that the matrix form is on the decline, and some companies such as Shell have indeed diluted their matrix, although they have not in any sense abandoned it – they are far too complex to manage without it. However, there is also a large number of major organizations that are moving more strongly towards a matrix structure, and Ford is an example of this trend.

In matrix organizations, the diffusion of responsibility is often accompanied by a very rapid set of movements of staff and bosses from project to project, location to location.

In these circumstances, the mentor can provide a useful contribution, giving individuals time to concentrate single-mindedly on their own development, but in a way that is deeply informed about the needs, urgencies and pressures of the organization. In an era of rapid change they can also provide a continuity, which may be lacking as line managers are changed and new projects come on stream. They can do this in part because mentoring is an occasional role, and, even if the learner and mentor are moved apart, they can still continue the relationship. Later in this book you will find a number of examples where this continuity has been afforded and has provided a source of stability in an otherwise uncomfortably fluid situation.

Some organizations have no stable line management structure for most of their employees. At Perot Systems, for example, most people work on projects. Over the course of a year, they may work for several project leaders, sometimes for more than one at a time. An off-line mentor provides a point of stability, someone to whom they can turn for authoritative advice. These mentors also, unusually, take responsibility for performance appraisal. Rather than sit in judgement, they collect and collate observations from the mentee's colleagues and project managers and feed this back in a supportive, developmental manner. The ICL Learning case (see pages 161-4) has a similar flavour.

The move towards learning companies

One of the main drivers in the quest for the learning company and the competitive advantage that learning can bring is the encouragement of individual responsibility. This responsibility is for taking the initiative around the work itself – not waiting to be told but getting on with what needs doing. As a conspicuously successful young civil servant said to one of us 'It is easier to apologise after than to seek permission before'.

Creating a learning company involves individuals taking responsibility not only for their work but also for their learning. They have to wean themselves from the dependence on the organization to doing development for them. For many people this will not come easy and it may need to be a staged process. Traditionally, full-time training and development people were charged with responsibility of others. In recent years there has been a call for line managers to become more involved. This process can be welcomed as progress, but line managers too have limits in terms of role and availability. The next stage in the weaning process could be seen as having the mentor support the individual, in a more hands-off way than the line manager might, but this is not the end of the chain. In a functioning learning company, there would be little need for appointed mentors because individuals would be running with the responsibility for doing it themselves. They may well have mentors as part of their network of growth, but they would manage the choosing, contracting and progressing of the relationship.

Schematically, the progression we have described looks like this:

Training department responsible $\rightarrow$ Line manager responsible $\rightarrow$ Mentor shares $\rightarrow$ Individuals responsible for themselves

The research in Motorola emphasises this importance of the learner in selecting the network of those who will help.

The ability of the mentor to help people gain insights is critical here. Insights may be personal (what motivates them; their strengths and weaknesses; how other people see them); or systematic (how things work here; what's the best way to get things done in these circumstances); or political (eg the nature and shape of organizational alliances). A model of the learning process we have developed elsewhere suggests that it is a cycle:

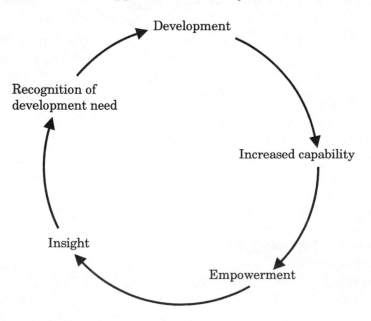

This cycle works equally for individuals, teams and whole organizations.

The new career paradigm

There are two points we wish to make about the new patterns for careers:

☐ careers in flattened and unstable modern organizations are less like a smooth escalator going up and more like a maze with blind alleys, secret gardens and underground tunnels

☐ there is still a need for people to move through to take leadership positions in organizations and there are now new routes to the top.

The career maze. In contemporary organizations each individual has more pressure on them to manage their own career. It has become a truism that companies can no longer offer even their core employees the promise of permanent employment. What is on offer at best is a promise to enhance employability. With less layers to rise through, more people will plateau earlier than in the past and will spend longer on one level. Many organizations used to hold out the promise of promotion almost as a substitute for taking seriously the development of individuals. This carrot is no longer so readily available.

The metaphor of the secret garden characterizes one feature of new careers. If people will not be moving up they need to be helped to find a place where they can experience adventure, challenge and growth without necessarily having a bigger job title.

There are also, as we suggested, underground tunnels. The trap doors that open into these tunnels are the envelopes left on the desk containing the P45 form to take to the unemployment benefit office. If organizations cannot guarantee employment then there is a moral and practical obligation to support the development of individual contributors so that they can sleep at nights in the knowledge that if they lose their job they are well equipped to handle the situation and find themselves something satisfying and rewarding to do.

Recent research by one of the authors has focused on the changes in routes to the top. The conclusions support the view that personalized assistance with career planning is increasingly a necessity. As people are obliged to work out their own paths through the maze, it helps to have a friendly sounding board, who can ideally take a broader perspective of the opportunities likely to open up within the organization.

Changing professional requirements

The British emphasis on the learning role of the mentor is encouraged by the pressure from National Vocational Qualifications and professional bodies moving towards competence-based development and accreditation of prior learning.

At the same time, professions such as personnel management increasingly recognize that achieving paper qualifications does not necessarily make someone confident and competent to practise. For the first few years, it helps greatly for them to have a more experienced practitioner, who can help them relate the theoretical to the practical and focus on broader career opportunities than just those on offer with their current employer.

WHAT IS A MENTOR?

We turn our attention now to the individual mentor and learner and the nature, skills and dynamics of their relationship.

One way of answering the question 'What is a mentor?' is by way of formal definition. Another is by the use of images. The image of the old, bearded, wise man in the Odyssey looking after the young prince, Telemachus, is quite well known. What is less well known is that Mentor in Homer's story is actually a form taken by the goddess Athene, thus neatly setting to one side any gender related image about mentors. Furthermore, when Odysseus returns from his wandering and he and his son Telemachus are faced with their final challenge, Athene, the mentor, did not:

> throw all her powers in, to give him victory, but continued to put the strength and courage of both Odysseus and Telemachus on trial, while she herself withdrew, taking the shape of a swallow and darting aloft to perch on the smoky beam of the hall. (Homer, 1964, p. 22)

The power of this image is that it puts mentors where they need to be, out of the action, looking on and encouraging, rather than taking over and doing the work for the learner. This is closer to the emerging British view of the role than some of the older images fostered in the USA.

An image of what mentoring is *not* comes from Caroline Altounyan's (1995) work where she talks of another Greek myth, about Procrustes. He lived in a cave and invited visitors in for a sumptuous banquet, with lots of wine. At the end of the evening he invited his tired and emotional visitors to stay the night. This is where the story gets nasty. If a visitor was too short for the bed, then Procrustes would put them on a rack to stretch them till they fitted better. If they were too long, then he chopped off the bits hanging over the end.

This image has two aspects. First, mentoring offers a rich banquet, and there are many different aspects of life and work that can be focused upon. Secondly, it is not our task, as mentors, to cut people down to the size that our preferences or the organization specification requires. Mentoring is too rich and individual for that: it is not a Procrustean bed.

Participants at the EMC/SBS mentoring research conference were asked to draw their own images of mentoring. From the range they drew, strong messages came about mentoring being about:

☐   big ears, small mouth

☐   finding the tune that the learner wants to play

☐   harmonizing the various contributors

☐   being in the delivery room, supporting new growth

☐   an upward, widening spiral

☐   seeing life as a tree, with roots as deep as the branches are high

☐   a 'Nellie', sitting alongside

☐   a laser beam

☐   a hand, a book and a boot

☐   a pebble in a still pool sending out ripples that extend in space and time.

All these images offer directions for us in considering what mentors might do. Often being connected to a visual image makes them more memorable too. These images all attest to the depth of the mentor's contribution. Having a mentor is an important developmental opportunity, not a fashion accessory.

Instructor, coach and mentor: some key distinctions

We can also become clearer about what mentoring is by attending to what it is not. The mentor stands distinct from either a coach or an instructor.

Instructors focus on the task, and their time perspective is a day or two. They show and tell, and give supervised practice: ownership of the relationship is with the instructor and they attempt to eliminate ambiguity.

The coach shifts the focus to the results of the job, and extends the time span of attention to months rather than days. They explore the problem with the learner and set up opportunities for the learner to try out new skills: ownership is shared and puzzling out ambiguity is seen as a challenge.

By contrast, mentors focus on the individual learner developing through their career or life. They act as friends willing to play the part of adversary in challenging assumptions, they listen and question to encourage the learner to widen their own view: they are happy for the ownership and direction of the relationship to lie with the learner and they accept ambiguity as an exciting part of life, providing the learner with the openings for change and autonomy.

The mentoring process

What do mentors do? Most successful mentoring relationships go through four phases. We describe these as:

1. establishing rapport (initiation)
2. direction setting (getting established)
3. progress making (development)
4. moving on (finalizing/maintenance).

Each of the phases has its own tasks, dynamics and skill requirements. We outline these below.

Mentoring works best when it is learner driven, so we are not attempting here to be prescriptive, and we expect that some relationships will take quite different paths driven by different urgencies. However, what follows describes the progress of a typical mentoring relationship.

Establishing rapport

Tasks. During this phase the mentor and the learner will:

☐ work out whether they can get on and respect each other

☐ exchange views on what the relationship is and is not

☐ agree a formal contract

☐ agree a way of working together

☐ set up a way of calling meetings, frequency, duration, location

☐ set up other contacts.

Dynamics. This phase can be characterised by:

☐ impatience to get going

☐ tentativeness and unwillingness to commit

☐ politeness

☐ testing out and challenging.

Skill requirements. In this phase the mentor may need to:

☐ suspend judgement

☐ be open to hints and unarticulated wishes or concerns

☐ be clear about what needs establishing and open about what can be left out

☐ establish a formal contract

☐ agree a way of working together

☐ set up details of future meetings

☐ achieve rapport.

Direction setting

Tasks. The mentor and the learner will:

- [ ] learn about the learner's style of learning
- [ ] think through the implications of their style for how they will work together
- [ ] diagnose needs
- [ ] determine learner's goals and initial needs
- [ ] set objective measures
- [ ] identify priority areas for work
- [ ] keep open space
- [ ] clarify focus of their work
- [ ] begin work.

Dynamics. Characteristic issues may include:

- [ ] over-inclination to shut down on possibilities
- [ ] unwillingness to set goals
- [ ] reluctance to open up possibilities for diagnosis.

Skill requirements. In addition to those mentioned earlier there will be:

- [ ] using and interpreting diagnostic frameworks and tools
- [ ] encouraging thinking through of implications of diagnoses
- [ ] setting up opportunities for diagnosis to be informed by third parties
- [ ] adopt developmental approach to goal setting for the learner
- [ ] help the selection of the initial area for work
- [ ] give feedback/set objectives/plan
- [ ] have clarity about the next step.

Progress making

Tasks. The mentor and the learner will:

☐ create a forum for progressing the learner's issues

☐ use each other's expertise as agreed

☐ establish a means for reviewing progress and adapting the process in the light of this review

☐ identify new issues and ways of working that are required

☐ be ready for the evolution of the relationship.

Dynamics. This phase will typically include:

☐ period of sustained productive activity

☐ dealing with a change in the relationship or the learner's circumstances

☐ reviewing and adapting the relationship

☐ preparing for moving on.

Skill requirements. This phase also requires:

☐ monitoring progress of learner

☐ relationship review and renegotiation

☐ recognizing achievements/objectives attained

☐ timing and managing the evolution of the relationship.

Moving on

Tasks. Now the mentor and the learner will:

☐ allow the relationship to end or evolve

☐ move to maintenance

☐ review what can be taken and used in other contexts.

Dynamics. This phase may include:

☐ dealing with rupture and loss

☐ major renegotiation and continuation

☐ evaluation and generalization.

Skills requirement. In this phase there may be a need to:

☐ address own and other's feelings of loss

☐ develop next phase and/or

☐ orchestrate a good ending

☐ think through and generalize learning

☐ establish friendship.

Determine the focus

It is worth bearing in mind that the presenting issue that the learner identifies may be only the first step towards the exploration of some deeper issue that they will not want to raise at first, or may not even be consciously aware of. This framework, therefore, serves to set out an agenda of possibilities for future attention.

The issues that the learner might want to discuss could be:

☐ focused on the organization's strategy and process

☐ focused on their role

☐ focused on a big task or project

☐ focused on particular skills

☐ focused upon development needs and career direction

☐ open – acting as sounding board.

An indication of which area a learner wishes to focus upon will come from the issues that they raised during the initiation and direction-setting stage. Some examples of the ways these issues are expressed are given below:

Organizational strategy and process

☐ I want to explore the organization's strategy

☐ I want to look at how we are organized

☐ I want to address how we are managed, eg quality issues, corporate responsibility, customer/supplier relations

☐ I want to improve the way we communicate in the organization

☐ I want to review how we work together and the performance of teams and individuals

☐ I want to get clearer about the environment we are working in and the competition we face.

Role

☐ I want to clarify what difference my new role makes to what I do

☐ I want to expand the possibilities of what I can do

☐ I want to resolve conflicts with other roles.

Big task or project

☐ I want to think through the benefits of this task/project

☐ I want to think through the formal and informal relationships I have and need in a major project

☐ I want to run my ideas for a major project in front of a dispassionate outsider

☐ I want to monitor my contribution to a major project.

Skills

☐ I want to get clear about what my strengths and weaknesses are

☐ I want to examine my own skills

☐ I want to build up specific skills, eg communication, decision-making, presentation.

Development needs and career

☐ I want to develop a plan for my own development in my current role

☐ I want to look beyond my current role

☐ I want to clarify what I am here to do, my purpose

☐ I want to look at how I can learn better from what happens

☐ I want to learn from my successes and failures.

Open space

☐ I want a sounding board

☐ I want time for me, and I am happy to see what comes up and run with it.

The focus can change over the life of a mentoring relationship, and this framework can provide guidance for mentors and learners seeking to keep an eye on the way the relationship is evolving.

Mutuality

Various authors on mentoring have made passing reference to the fact that mentors also learn, but there has been relatively little analysis of *what* and *how* they learn from the relationship. This is a theme that has preoccupied one of the authors for some time and is the subject of on-going research. Sufficient feedback has been gathered to provide some straightforward observations, however.

Mentors gain from their mentees:

☐ Insights into new areas of skill/technology. (Younger people are frequently much more adept at using computer functions, for example.)

☐ An opportunity to evaluate critically the intuitive processes they use. To explain their thinking to the mentee they often have to articulate subconscious processes and open them up for critical discussion and reflection.

☐   The benefit of matching experience-based advice against what happens when the mentee follows it.

☐   A stimulus to review their own knowledge and learning of topics that come up for discussion.

☐   Clues to hidden issues that their own direct reports will not broach with them. As one group of learners in cross-cultural mentoring relationships put it: 'the mentor will learn about the little things that frustrate us and recognize that he may be frustrating his own people'.

There are benefits for the mentor outside the learning framework. Surveys conducted by the authors have invariably identified 'satisfaction in seeing someone else grow' as the principal benefit mentors perceive. This psychosocial gratification is reinforced if the learner acknowledges the debt.

As the relationship matures, the mentor may find that the giving of support becomes increasingly mutual. The partners use each other as sounding boards. In the cross-cultural case referred to above, mentors began to ask their learners questions such as: 'How do you think a Malay audience would react to this?'

A CODE OF ETHICS FOR MENTORING

The rapid spread of applications of mentoring has increasingly raised the issue of proper conduct by mentor and learner. Some generic guidelines have always been present in formal business mentoring schemes – for example, the importance of strict confidentiality and for the learner to avoid misusing the mentor's authority. Less clear, however, are issues such as:

☐   Where are the boundaries of what can be discussed?

☐   To what extent should the mentor attempt to drive the learner towards a particular action or decision?

☐   In a conflict of interest between the mentor and the learner, where should the mentor's priorities lie?

Mentoring Directors, an organization specializing in the provision of external mentors for senior executives, has developed a code of practice for its mentors, and we expect this practice to spread. At the very least, it will provide a useful starting point for discussion in organizations wishing to establish their own guidelines.

SUMMARY

Two trends are happening simultaneously in mentoring. One is that the application of the technique is spreading well beyond the business/professional boundaries, creating exciting new opportunities to learn from schemes that begin from very different perspectives. The other is that the focus for innovation in research and application of business mentoring has shifted from North America to the UK and Europe.

As a result, a whole range of issues and options has opened up, stimulating an explosion of research and experimentation. Some of the experiments are reported in the cases in this book – but these represent only a small proportion of the innovation going on.

References

Altounyan C (1995) 'Putting mentors in their place: the role of workplace support in professional education', MSc HRM Dissertation, Sheffield Business School, Sheffield.

Boydell T, Leary M, Megginson D and Pedler M (1991) *Developing the Developers*, AMED, London.

Caruso R E (1992) *Mentoring and the Business Environment: Asset or Liability?* Dartmouth, Aldershot.

Gibb S and Megginson D (1993) 'Inside corporate mentoring schemes: a new agenda of concerns', *Personnel Review* 22(1), 40–54.

Homer (trans. E V Rieu) (1964) *The Odyssey*, Penguin, Harmondsworth.

Industrial Society (1992) Training Report No. 4, Industrial Society, London.

Megginson D, Clutterbuck D and Whitaker V (1994) 'Conclusions from the conference', Proceedings of the EMC/SBS Mentoring Research Conference, European Mentoring Centre, UK.

PART 2
Organization Cases

2
CASE STUDIES

INTRODUCTION

The following cases illustrate a wide spectrum of approaches to the development of formal mentoring in a variety of organizations and sectors, both private and public. They are predominantly British examples, although they include one each from Sweden and France. This is no accident; mentoring is considerably more established in the UK than in the rest of Europe.

In reading these cases, you may well be struck, as we were, by common threads such as the need for training of mentors (and often learners). You will also find that mentoring appears to be of value to people at all ages and walks of life, from the young to the old, from the able-bodied to the disabled, from the very junior to the very senior. It really does seem that *everyone needs a mentor*, at some time in their lives.

I. THE 'BEAT' PROJECT FOR YOUNG OFFENDERS IN BIRMINGHAM*

Coral Gardiner

Emerging from talks between the West Midlands Probation Service and the Birmingham Training and Enterprise Council was the need for a new and innovative project to move individuals out of the criminal justice system into education, training and employment. Resulting from this need came the idea of using a mentor as a means of support. In May 1993 the seed began to grow. The project was called BEAT (Beginning Employment and Training) and the means of support was via a mentoring system.

The project objectives

Aims and objectives were set up and strategies developed to put in place a framework for action.

The aims were to develop and implement programmes to increase the *personal* and *vocational* effectiveness of young people (offenders) identified by the Probation Service, and also to assist young offenders (16–18 years) to develop realistic career plans, increase take-up of Training Credits, and improve levels of success in placements in employment and further education and training.

The process included the carrying out of needs assessment, access to careers education and identification, and recruitment and training of mentors. The project also required systems to be set up and processes for monitoring, reviewing and evaluation.

The backdrop

Beginning employment and training is not always the priority for a young offender. Offending covers a vast range of crime, from violence to fraud, dishonesty to error. Although one in three men are convicted of a criminal offence by the age of 30 (Home Office

---

*   © Copyright: BEAT

estimate), the offences are predominately committed by those under 25. Half of these offenders are under 21.

To begin to overcome the barriers facing young offenders there is an obvious need to understand what these barriers are, along with having an insight into the needs of the offender. It is clear that unemployment and crime are linked, directly or indirectly, and research studies have highlighted the following:

☐ unemployment is a significant cause of crime, particularly among young men who already have a criminal record

☐ employment and training are of great value in reducing the likelihood of re-offending

☐ young men from minority ethnic communities are disproportionately more likely to be in contact with the criminal justice system.

The employment prospects for young men as a whole are worsening and especially so for young offenders. The current developments in the labour market include:

☐ a sustained loss of jobs generally

☐ a shift from unskilled to skilled and multi-skilled work

☐ a shift from manufacturing/construction industries to the service sector

☐ a shift from full-time to part-time and from secure to temporary contract work

☐ a loss of income support for 16 and 17 year olds

☐ fewer training and education opportunities.

The fundamentals

The following questions had to be answered for such a mentoring system to succeed.

1. Why mentoring?
2. How and who would coordinate the system?
3. How and where would the mentors come from?
4. What are the appropriate systems for setting up monitoring, review and evaluation?

5. What will be in the mentor development programme?
6. Will it meet the organization's objectives?
7. What are the needs of the participants and how will all the parties benefit?
8. Is there commitment from the top?

The partnership

As a pilot project BEAT was supported by a number of project partners who all shared an interest in the development of the system:

The West Midlands Probation Service wished to make a response to the growing numbers of youth crime cases, the 16-18 year olds being the most vulnerable.

Birmingham TEC wanted to ensure access was made available to ex-offenders for government funded provision, namely pre-vocational courses and training credits.

The Careers Service wanted to ensure access to careers education and guidance as a means of informing choices.

The City Council's economic development department wanted to observe mentoring as a potential tool to benefit other citizens across the city.

The framework

The mentor recruitment and selection process involved advertising from within the local community, shortlisting from application forms, a day-long interview programme and half a day of project induction.

From then on we had an action learning project where mentors came together regularly with the coordinator to work in sets to solve the issues of the day. As this was the only mentoring system of its kind within the UK Probation Service, we were collectively participating in a piece of action research. Young people were recruited on a voluntary basis on the recommendation of their probation officer and they came forward independently for their initial contact with BEAT. At this stage the young people were offered the choice of the cultural background and gender of their mentor.

The system was monitored and reviewed by the coordinator using statistical analysis, monthly reports and verbal feedback from mentor development sessions.

The project ethos

The project's cultural values were built around the person-centred concept (Rogers 1961) and took an holistic approach towards participants and everyone involved with the project.

The starting point – the participants

Initial research was carried out to establish expressed needs and perceived and actual barriers to success. They are as follows:

Expressed needs

☐ to develop a sense of self respect/self awareness/self worth

☐ to develop self confidence

☐ to have guidance and advice on career routes and progression

☐ to have information about how to access systems, eg DSS, housing department

☐ to have information on how to access chosen options

☐ to have the opportunity to develop occupational skills in a safe environment

☐ to gain experience of the world of work

☐ to have some form of regular income

☐ to have access to counselling on personal problems and on training problems

☐ to have the chance to develop basic skills

☐ to be treated fairly

☐ to gain advice on the disclosure of convictions

☐ to be recognized for current abilities.

Perceived/actual barriers

☐ marginalization at school

☐ lack of skills and experience

☐ lack of information to inform choices

☐ the perceptions of others

☐ poor view of training

☐ criminal record.

Analysing the problem

A SWOT analysis was carried out to analyse the problems faced by the young offender accessing the system.

Strengths

Each individual brings unique elements to the development of the project.

Weaknesses

Participants had:

1. no previous history of training for the world of work
2. vulnerability to re-offend due to peer group pressure
3. lack of money
4. low self-esteem
5. lack of appropriate job opportunities.

Opportunities

1. the opportunity to succeed via the BEAT project
2. the chance to try out new things via training programmes
3. the opportunity for career planning
4. the opportunity to develop towards realistic employment goals
5. the opportunity to have a personal mentor as a role model.

Threats

1. organizations and systems may try to create barriers to success
2. other people's perceptions
3. pressures from peers or circumstances to re-offend.

The mentors

Mentors were drawn from all walks of life and underwent training and development in the following mentor-specific skills:

☐ active listening

☐ empathy

☐ counselling

☐ negotiation

☐ coaching

☐ advocacy

☐ problem solving

☐ decision making

☐ reflection and review

☐ constructive feedback

☐ interpersonal skills

☐ verbal and non-verbal communication.

They also had specific training in the criminal justice system.

The art of mentoring is in knowing which skills are applicable and in which order of priority for any given scenario.

Mentors relate the use of counselling skills to the process of empowerment as the diagram demonstrates. Mentors also relate to Maslow's motivation theory. Many of the young people whom they mentor on a one-to-one basis are on the base line of Maslow's hierarchy. They have basic survival needs, eg accommodation, money. Mentors work with young people to encourage a sense of self-respect and worth.

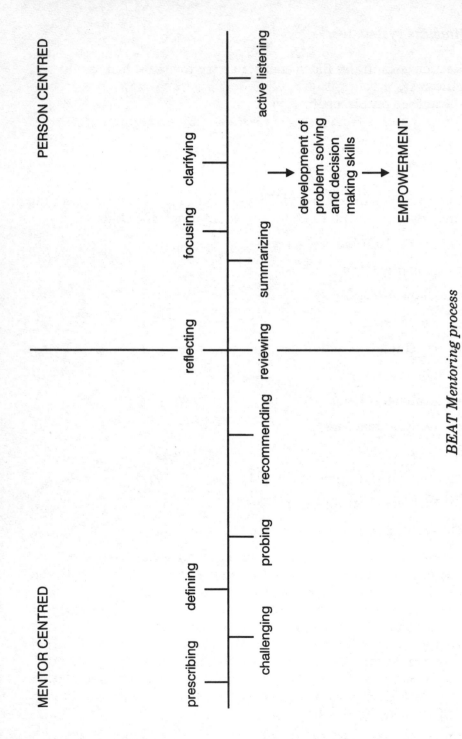

MENTOR CENTRED

PERSON CENTRED

prescribing   defining   probing   recommending   reflecting   summarizing   focusing   clarifying   active listening

challenging

reviewing

development of problem solving and decision making skills → EMPOWERMENT

BEAT Mentoring process

How the system works

Participants in the BEAT project are referred by their probation officer via a referral form. The flow diagram shows the process through to outcome:

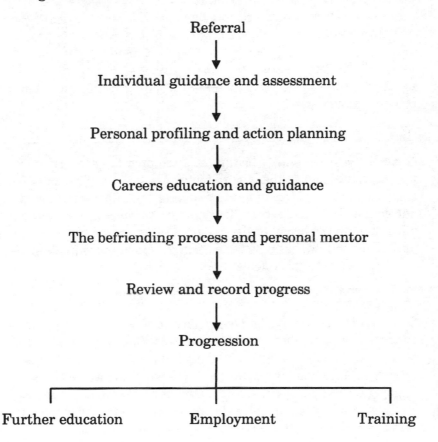

Referral

↓

Individual guidance and assessment

↓

Personal profiling and action planning

↓

Careers education and guidance

↓

The befriending process and personal mentor

↓

Review and record progress

↓

Progression

Further education   Employment   Training

The benefits

The benefits of the system are wide ranging. The following case studies demonstrate benefits to individuals.

S is an 18-year-old mentored by a mature female. He approached BEAT on leaving prison with a history of burglary and assault. With the aid of his mentor he gained a training place and shortly afterwards was offered a work placement. Within the year he obtained his NVQ level 2 qualification in bench joinery and accepted an offer of permanent employment with his placement. At one stage in his development this all seemed beyond his hopes. S was accused of stealing and had to attend an identity parade at the local police station. With the intervention and support of his personal mentor he was able to deal with the false accusations and charges were dropped.

G is a 17-year-old with a history of attempted burglary. He now lives with his grandmother due to family breakdown. His mentor is a manager in a manufacturing company. He made enquiries at work and found that there were a few current vacancies. The mentor advocated on G's behalf to the personnel section and obtained an application form. G has now been offered a job at the workplace of the mentor due to this intervention.

D has a spent conviction. She has been out of work for three years. When she was accepted to BEAT she was looking for work. The co-ordinator knew of a temporary vacancy for a Maths and English teacher within a training organization. D applied and was successful in going on to permanent employment one year later. D had low levels of confidence and self-esteem, which mentor development sessions and networking were able to help her address.

Benefits to young people

The intervention of a mentor offers the young person the opportunity to:

1.   raise self-esteem, self-respect and thus self-confidence
2.   gain confidence in their own ability enabling them to shape their own life chances

3. increase communication skills – ie more confidence in the use of non-verbal, written and verbal communication
4. develop core skills enabling a greater understanding of 'self' in the context of the wider society
5. develop greater motivation and determination to succeed
6. demonstrate what can be achieved
7. achieve greater independence – increased decision making, organization, planning and problem solving skills
8. set own goals and gain a sense of achievement through moving on
9. become a positive role model
10. develop self-pride and sense of worth.

Benefits to mentors

These stated benefits were established by group and individual evaluation.

1. able to transfer knowledge to work and personal situations
2. more able to analyse problems
3. development of listening skills
4. raised expectations of self and young person being mentored
5. a sense of achievement
6. greater communications skills
7. more self-analytical
8. greater sense of 'self'
9. more aware of the perceptions of others
10. the development of intuition
11. more able to assist in the decision-making processes for self and in the use of guidance to the young person
12. raised self-esteem
13. more self-empowerment gaining through the processes (mentoring and development sessions)
14. development of patience and tolerance
15. more motivated
16. greater confidence
17. more influential to the benefit of others
18. increased personal effectiveness
19. increased interpersonal skills

20. more focused
21. more highly developed, mentor-specific skills.

Benefits to training providers, employers and colleges

By networking effectively with these organizations the project and the mentors are able to advocate on behalf of the ex-offender. Through working together they are able to gain a greater understanding of the barriers facing offenders. Thus they are equipping other organizations to be aware of the barriers they create and how to develop appropriate strategies to ensure fair and equal access for young ex-offenders.

Benefits to probation officers

1. probation officers have found satisfaction in seeing young people on their case loads moving forward into training and employment
2. communication enhancement with the young person, the mentor and the probation officer forming a three-way relationship. This is particularly useful for informing the courts
3. Observing the young person developing confidence in themselves, lessening the likelihood of their re-offending.

The lessons

1. Barriers to the take-up of training by young offenders were identified at a number of key points:
    — in the attitude and confidence of young offenders in the youth training system. This included resignation, despair and hostility to training opportunities
    — lack of confidence, self-esteem and other personal and social problems that inhibited access and progression
    — in the practice of agencies in the criminal justice system
    — in the training system; although again there were many examples of good provision, there was also some resistance, suspicion and concern by employment and training providers about their ability to meet the needs of the young offender.

Although there were many examples of group work practice, assessment, information-giving and motivational work, the referral system by staff in the prison, probation and social services was patchy during the first year.

2. The project demonstrated that many of these problems can be overcome by:
   — better assessment and guidance of the young offender through the mentoring system
   — programmes of supervision that integrate employment work more centrally into the supervision process of the probation service
   — awareness-raising and training of staff in the criminal justice agencies and in the employment and training agencies
   — training programmes that can recognize and respond to any special needs of the young offender
   — closer working links between staff in criminal justice agencies (particularly the probation service), staff in the careers service, and training providers.

There have also been some important lessons from the experience of mentoring on the project that need attention for future good practice.

1. Whilst mentors must view the expectations of the young person with enthusiasm, a balanced outlook of what is a realistically achievable goal for the young person is critical to the success of all the parties.
2. The mentoring system's potential pitfall is that of a mismatch of mentor to young person. This can be unhelpful for both the young person and the mentor.

   The key role of the mentor coordinator is to draw on professional expertise and experience to know both parties well enough to get a 'best fit' situation.
3. Mentoring requires key skills:
   — active listening
   — empathy
   — counselling
   — negotiation
   — coaching
   — advocacy
   — problem solving

- decision making
- reflection and review
- constructive feedback
- interpersonal skills
- verbal and non-verbal communication.

The lesson is knowing which skills are applicable and in which order of priority in any given scenario.

Key findings

Of the total number of young people referred there was an approximate 50 : 50 ratio of individuals from minority ethnic communities to individuals of White/European origin.

Of those progressing beyond the initial referral, two thirds were of minority ethnic community to one third White/European.

Of those from minority ethnic backgrounds:

☐   75 per cent were Black African/Caribbean

☐   23 per cent were Asian

☐   2 per cent were of mixed race.

These dramatic findings indicate that young Black people have participated on the premise:

☐   that they want a mentor

☐   that they have valued an ongoing mentoring relationship.

It is significant that of those staying on the project there is a larger number from minority ethnic communities.

The project has demonstrated that those taking part in the mentoring process are less likely to fail and are more likely to succeed. Records indicate that they are not known to be re-offending.

Approximately half of those taking part are in employment, training or education. The project has reached a significant number of young people who had previously not progressed to the training systems available.

Costs and benefits

The cost of a young person participating in the BEAT project is £22 per week. The cost of holding a young person in custody is £440 per week.

Discussion

Focus for vulnerable learners. Mentoring can be at its most powerful when it is aimed at vulnerable members of society. While there clearly is a learning context to these relationships, the emphasis will inevitably be on support, on raising confidence and the mentee's sense of self-worth.

Mutuality. The mutuality of the mentoring relationship also comes across strongly. These mentors gave and received a great deal from the experience.

References

Maslow, A H (1992) *Towards a Psychology of Being*, Van Norstrand, New York.

Rogers, C R (1961) *On Becoming a Person*, Houghton Mifflin, Boston.

2. NATIONAL MENTORING CONSORTIUM'S SCHEME FOR BLACK UNDERGRADUATES

Norman McLean, Director, Mentor Unit, National Mentoring Consortium

Mentoring is not new to Black people, in fact it thrives naturally in societies outside the West. The original University of East London mentor scheme was launched in 1992 to meet the needs of African, Caribbean and Asian undergraduates. Recent research has shown that Black graduates are twice as likely to be unemployed as their White counterparts, that they are likely to be more highly qualified, that they have to make more applications before obtaining interviews and that they feel that employers do not value their experiences and culture.

Without generalizing, many African and Asian students lack information about recruitment practices and how to succeed. Many need encouragement to apply to prestigious employers: some are the first in their family undertaking higher education and have no careers advice from their communities. When discrimination is added, stress and isolation increase. The mentor scheme addresses these issues: participating organizations have noted considerable improvements in the attitudes towards, and on the part of, Black and Asian students.

Such was the success of the original scheme that the University of East London was joined in 1994 by universities in other parts of the country to form the National Mentoring Consortium.

The scheme

The National Mentoring Consortium prepares and develops high-calibre African, Caribbean and Asian undergraduates for successful recruitment into graduate management training schemes. It does this by matching students in one-to-one relationships with mentors from supporting companies. The scheme is designed to improve the confidence and self-image of African, Caribbean and Asian undergraduates, mainly in the second and third years of their degree courses.

Recruitment and piloting

Students were attracted to the scheme by presentations to their academic departments and societies, and poster campaigns. Employers and other participating universities were recruited mainly by direct approach and by articles in the national, community and specialist press.

A pilot mentor scheme was launched in 1992 to cater for 30 students. Such was the demand that 50 places were provided with the support of 25 employers. The national scheme that started in 1994 is in itself a pilot project that will be fully evaluated after three years.

Mentors are selected by participating employers according to guidelines produced centrally. Mentors should be responsible people within their organizations, and can be graduates themselves. Up to 1994, all mentors were African, Caribbean or Asian, but with the launch of the national scheme, White members were also included.

Mentees are asked to complete an application form, and then attend a short interview with members of the Mentor Unit staff. Students are selected according to the benefits that it is considered the scheme will provide for them – in practice, very few applicants are unsuccessful.

Matching mentor and mentee

Students and mentors are usually matched according to professional discipline and career interests, and to a lesser extent by gender. In some instances students may opt to work with a White mentor. The pairs are introduced to each other at an introductory evening which marks the beginning of their relationship.

Guidance, training and support

All mentoring partnerships operate according to guidelines set out by the National Mentoring Consortium. The pair meet for a minimum of half-a-day per month for four to six months, usually in the mentor's workplace. The successful completion of the process is marked at the annual award ceremony where mentors and students receive certificates.

All mentors are required to attend a training programme that consists of compulsory and optional elements. All are required to attend an induction session and the introduction session where students and mentors meet for the first time. In addition, training is offered in coaching skills for mentoring, counselling skills for mentoring and dealing with difficult mentoring situations; mentors are required to attend at least two of these sessions.

Each mentor is paired with another mentor, and each student with another student for mutual support and encouragement. Support is also available from local scheme co-ordinators or from the central mentor unit at the University of East London. A network group is being established initially in London for mentors and students that will provide opportunities to meet socially and to network. The group will address issues of isolation, seek resolution to organizational issues and provide support and the opportunity to share issues of mutual concern. Mentors and students receive a handbook produced by the National Mentoring Consortium, which contains full information and suggestions for further reading.

Objectives and structure

The mentoring process begins when the mentoring pair agree an individual learning contract, which provides a framework for the work undertaken within the relationship.

A central office in the Mentor Unit at the University of East London coordinates the management of the scheme including training of staff, production of publicity materials and fundraising. Each university provides a coordinator, administrative support and a contribution towards the funding. Liaison officers support the university staff in running induction events, working with local employers and general administration.

Measuring the success

The success of each relationship is measured largely by the pairs themselves through a learning contract, peer group evaluation mid-way, questionnaire and report at the end. A major indicator is the extent to which the agreed learning objectives of the students are met.

The scheme is seen as an important equal opportunities initiative, helping both higher education institutions and employers to ensure fair treatment for their clients, whether they are undergraduates or graduate recruits. All students and mentors attend a mid-term evaluation evening, which aims to address any difficulties and to pinpoint areas for improvement. Students provide a formal assessment of their learning outcomes in an end-of-scheme report. This report is an important tool in appraisal, inviting the student to engage in self-assessment, exercising skills of evaluation, analysis and judgement. Mentors are also required to write a short report, or the pair may agree to produce a joint report.

Participants have given the scheme very favourable evaluations. In 1992-93, 80 per cent reported that they had found the scheme 'valuable' or 'very valuable'. In 1993-94, over 90 per cent of mentors found the scheme 'challenging, rewarding and valuable'. Eighty-five per cent of student participants felt that their time on the scheme had enhanced their personal development, and 89 per cent felt that their self-confidence had also improved.

The NMC is seeking funding from the Commission for Racial Equality for research to provide a longitudinal evaluation of the scheme, using case studies and quantitative and qualitative analysis.

In general there have been very few problems that have not been solved fairly quickly given the positive attitudes and enthusiasm engendered in the training and the determination and goodwill of those involved. There are only difficulties when one of the partners is unable to meet their commitments, through illness or other pressures of work or study.

Integration with other aspects of development

The mentor scheme is designed to meet the personal and professional needs of undergraduates. As such it fits well with other aspects of students' degree work. We are working on ways of accrediting the work that students undertake while on the scheme so that they receive formal academic recognition for this very important aspect of their studies.

The management development workshops that mentors receive in coaching skills, counselling skills and dealing with difficult situations is very relevant to their roles as managers. We are also examining the possibility of accrediting mentors for their work through the framework of National Vocational Qualifications.

Limitations

While the mentoring relationship is a very powerful tool for enhancing personal and professional development, it cannot hope to solve every problem that is brought to it. It is time constrained and bounded by the aims and objectives established in the individuals' learning contracts. Perhaps most importantly, it cannot guarantee an end result such as placement into employment, where this is governed by outside factors.

Discussion

Clear aims. It is important that the aims and objectives of any mentoring scheme are clearly stated and understood and accepted by all participants. This is to avoid dissatisfaction when unreasonable expectations are not met.

Support and training. Mentoring is not an automatic process, and it is not sufficient to put two people together and expect them to forge a productive relationship. Care needs to be taken with professional and rigorous preparation of both mentor and mentee, so that both enter the process adequately trained and briefed as to what is expected of them, and what realistically they may expect to gain from the experience.

Cross-race mentoring. Whereas many Black mentees value having a Black mentor, others are happy to work with a White mentor.

3. A PILOT YEAR OF MENTORING STUDENTS AT A FRENCH BUSINESS SCHOOL*

Liz Borredon, EDHEC, Lille, France

How we prepare students for management and entrepreneurship is a major debate common to all business schools in Europe as they seek to respond to the challenge of internationalization, competition and a changing environment.

In designing new learning programmes, schools turn to new technology, distance learning, and networking in order to secure their own position as well as to develop conditions that will provide for future needs of both organizations and society at large.

New skills are necessary; the skill base is both technical and human. Subject specific material will benefit from knowledge-based research supported by technologically aided communication.

Intellectual capital, however, cannot meet future needs if it is isolated from continuous learning and the capacity for working with others. The challenge is to develop individuals who are clear thinking, culturally unbiased and flexible; and to allow the naturally strong, wise, and perceptive qualities to emerge.

While the issues remain the same, the response varies. In the UK for example, the challenge is being met by a variety of mentoring programmes. In France, the challenge is different. Where the UK has a tradition of personal tutoring and 'low power distance', France has a tradition of a more rational nature with a 'high power distance' (Hofstede 1991). In France, those seeking to integrate personal competencies and behavioural skills into programme designs would be pioneering new territory.

In 1994 a business school in France launched a pilot project with the specific aim of broadening students' learning to include personal development and preparation for more perceptive leadership.

---

*   This project could not have progressed without the contribution and collaboration of my colleague, Professor Gérard Désmuliers.

This chapter describes how this project was initiated, and the stages through which it progressed. It then explains the present and on-going work in finding the school's unique response to complementing academic excellence.

EDHEC Graduate Business School is France's largest *Grande Ecole* in its domain. The *Grandes Ecoles* have no direct equivalent in other Western educational systems. They are private centres of learning that prepare their students for careers in either engineering, the civil service or business. Where French universities are open to all who possess a baccalaureate, the *Grandes Ecoles*, renowned for their academic excellence, are the preserve of a fee paying *élite* who have spent two years after their 'bac' preparing for a highly competitive entrance exam. Out of the 1666 eligible applicants in June 1994 for example, EDHEC selected 406 students for the present three-year programme at their Lille and Nice campuses.

Traditionally students have considered a *Grande Ecole* to be a certain passport to their future career. Once through the doors, there is a tendency for students to feel they have 'made it'; all that remains is to select their post and the sector of activity.

The start of mentoring at EDHEC

In 1993 EDHEC was placed in the league of the first five business schools in France. The recently opened Nice campus was well established. The school had growing portfolios of international student exchange programmes.

Feedback from the large and medium-sized companies who often recruit graduates from the *Grandes Ecoles* indicated an increasing need for preparing future executives who were adaptable, open minded, flexible and able to lead and work in teams.

Advocates of the so-called 'soft skills' would have difficulty in having them accepted in the traditional rational system that characterizes French management schools. Typically, both students and staff find such notions either 'too personal' or 'too obvious' to be part of programmes offered.

The school's mission statement called for a creative joint effort in responding to this new challenge. I volunteered to research mentoring with a view to setting up a project at the school.

I contacted organizations who had mentoring programmes or staff development schemes. I also contacted centres in the UK who had tutor schemes in the hope of developing a network.

I talked with heads of department and colleagues at EDHEC. I was told that what I called mentoring could not work; that it was of passing interest; that we could not allocate time in an over-stretched programme. It was suggested that it was not my place to discuss programme development with heads of department, and to leave strategic issues to people with more responsibility in the school. At the opposite extreme I was also encouraged by those committed to the students' personal progress.

Although enthusiasm was by no means universal, I believed it was a matter of finding the appropriate *form*, for what was a response to a real need within the school.

At the beginning of September 1993 I intended to continue my desk research once the school-year formalities had subsided. Apart from preparing new courses, there was a three-day staff seminar to attend.

The theme of the staff seminar in September 1993 was 'Working together Creatively'. At a workshop session 16 of us – administrative officers, teachers and secretaries – worked on preparing a proposal in response to the question: 'How can we favour personal student supervision when student numbers are increasing?'

Our proposal for a pilot project

At the end of the workshop, two of us prepared for presenting our group proposal to the executive committee. My colleague was a finance professor with whom I had not spoken prior to the seminar. Our aim was to find an appropriate vehicle for personal student supervision. The research project had ceased to be a personal undertaking.

We called our intended personal supervision 'mentoring'. In mentoring we were concerned about 'dialogue' with the student; dialogue that could take any number of forms, but whose purpose was to help the student:

☐ step back and see their development in perspective

☐   define objectives and review progress towards defining their career project.

We wanted to make a distinction between mentoring and subject tutoring. An academic orientation would have the project reinforce 'teaching' in the traditional sense. We were looking for a different type of exchange that was nevertheless pedagogical. This was our primary concern when making our proposal to the executive committee and the focus for our personal work in formulating our request.

We positioned mentoring as a response to personal student supervision. The mentor is a pedagogue. Just as Pedagos, the Greek slave, accompanied children to the place where learning took place, so the mentor, a trusted guide, accompanies the student to the point where there is learning or discovery. Another way of presenting the same notion is in LA Machando's words, *On ne peut rien enseigner: on peut que faciliter les moyens d'apprendre* (We cannot teach anything; we can but facilitate the learning process).

In order to complement academic excellence and subject-specific knowledge, we proposed developing personal competencies that would help students to lead, inspire, cooperate with others and adapt to changing environments. We wanted to focus on concern for 'being' as well as concern for 'doing'.

In order to achieve our aim, we proposed:

☐   setting up a mentoring (personal tutor) system

☐   developing ourselves as a group of mentors (personal tutors)

☐   learning from each other and those who had mentored or tutored before.

 Mentors would be any member of EDHEC staff who wanted to contribute in the spirit of confidentiality and respect.

The target group was all first-year students at the EDHEC Lille campus; the one-to-one mentoring relationship was to be for the three years the students remained at EDHEC.

The executive committee agreed to our proposal. We were given the go-ahead to launch personal tutoring for first-year EDHEC students as a pilot scheme under the umbrella of the newly created *Ateliers de Recherche et Creation, ARC projects* (Research and Creativity Workshops).

Although the 16 members of the original discussion group were interested, they were not all available to take the next step, assuming we knew what the next step was. We needed to bring sufficient tutors together in order to prepare for a one-to-one relationship with all 300 first-year students at EDHEC Lille.

At this stage, I discontinued my desk research; we had become engaged in the practical challenge of setting up the project. I felt able to share the work I had done in the UK on 'Introducing Counselling Skills', believing that trust in the inherent wisdom of the learner with his or her latent capacity for finer perceptions lay at the heart of mentoring.

The 'Charter' and first workshops

There were several workshops for those interested in the project. In all, 30 members of staff with different functions and levels of seniority participated.

There were three parts to the workshop:

1. developing a common understanding of mentoring as well as establishing shared objectives
2. defining our needs in order to launch the project
3. agreeing on practical procedures for establishing contact with 'mentees'.

The workshops were sufficiently small for us to remain in plenary. We questioned, collected every contribution and then assembled ideas in clusters. We used 'MagNotes', hexagons which adhere magnetically to whiteboards and can be moved around, finishing up with a model or joint mind-map of everyone's contribution.

Together we established the purpose of mentoring as 'Helping the student develop personal competencies in self management, interpersonal skills and creative thinking'.

Figure 1 shows a more detailed response to the question: What does a mentor do?

What we were aiming at was very different to the traditional concern in French business schools for developing subject knowledge with the teacher as 'expert'.

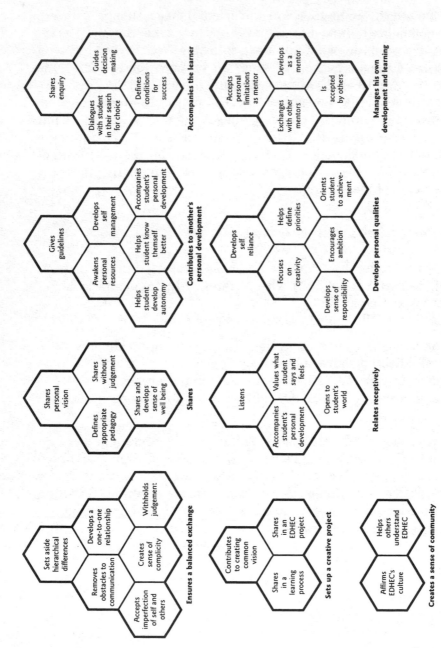

Figure 1 *What does a mentor do?*

At this stage the greatest need expressed by participants was for having adequate information and documentation on EDHEC and student associations.

There was no apparent enthusiasm for training. I realized that a counselling workshop was of little interest and indeed counter cultural. Although our objective was shared and developed together, there was a gap between these objectives and our personal experience of mentoring or being mentored.

Before finalizing our charter, we agreed on the practicalities for launching the project, which we were to discuss with students. As there were 25 mentors, it meant each one would have between 10 and 11 'mentees'.

The Charter

A mentor at EDHEC is someone who chooses to be so.

Mentoring is a voluntary engagement and non remunerative; under no condition can it be imposed on either mentor or student.

Mentoring is not the exclusive prerogative of teaching staff; the requirement for being a mentor rests on acceptance of this charter.

Mentoring is based on strict confidentiality and respect.

The basis of mentoring is establishing a relationship of mutual trust. The exchange between student and mentor concerns only those two individuals.

Mentors are not alone in their work. There will be a support group.

While mentoring requires confidentiality and respect, mentors will be asked to exchange personal learning in order that all concerned can further their work.

Parrainage (godparenting)

Four of us met with student representatives to explain our work to date and to get initial feedback. The notion of mentoring was not familiar to them, but they were not against it. The longest part of our discussion was around the term 'mentor'. Students did not care for this word or for 'personal tutor', they preferred the term *parrainage*. This means godparenting.

We explained we would, arbitrarily, link one mentor with ten students. Each student would receive a letter informing them of the project, giving the name of their *parrain* and a date for the first meeting.

The letter described *parrainage* as a pilot scheme with two aims: the first to give the opportunity for a more personal, individual relationship with a permanent member of EDHEC staff, the second, through dialogue with a *parrain*, to reach a clearer view of their professional project and how best to prepare for it. Each *filleul* (godchild) was given the name of their *parrain*, the date, time and place of their first meeting. It was made clear that the relationship, based on respect and confidentiality, was voluntary on both parts.

Of the 300 students in the first year, 152 responded. Between February and May 1994 the 25 *parrains* saw between two to six of the ten *filleuls* with whom they were coupled. Half of these returned a second time and a third of the students, three or more times. All administrative staff found their *filleuls* did not return a second time, while the response to teaching staff was mixed.

Broadening understanding of parrainage

During the preparatory workshops we had identified areas of competency or generic skill we hoped to develop in our students. I looked into the Behavioural Event Interview (BEI), a process of identifying personal qualities that can be used to specify a professionally sought-after level of maturity. (McBer group and Harvard University, USA).

There was potential in training *parrains* in conducting the BEI test with a student and then using the results as a launch pad for further dialogue. Information on this was circulated to *parrains* in order to discuss responses at our review meeting.

I learnt of the work of Jean Motte, a managing director who, outside of his official professional function, had set up an association and *parrainage* to help unemployed *cadres*. He also piloted seminars for potential managers about to enter the market, believing that a professional project would remain an intellectual exercise unless students were given the opportunity to reflect on experience and vocational inclination.

It was clear that the underlying necessities were respect, trust, empathy, listening and self disclosure; without this base, the seminar could not have had the very positive results Jean described.

It seemed to me that we were closer to an alternative way of learning how to facilitate the learner's personal discovery. Jean Motte agreed to come to our next meeting.

Reviewing the experience

We were now in May 1994. Almost all EDHEC *parrains* met for a half-day review of the pilot mentoring project. We werc 30 in total. Apart from *parrains*, we were joined by others who had become interested over the trial period.

The purpose of this meeting was to:

☐ review the strengths and weaknesses of the pilot project to date

☐ identify learning so that the project could evolve

☐ identify unresolved areas and needs

☐ make recommendations for the following year

☐ to welcome Jean Motte and hear of his approach to *parrainage* and professional projects

☐ discuss the appropriateness of the BEI at EDHEC.

The BEI appeared to be too threatening. Most felt it required psychological training; the group did not think they could be prepared for this work, believing it to be too specialized.

Jean Motte was greatly appreciated for his straightforwardness. I discovered that my colleagues favour what is called *temoignage* (personal testimony).

For the review of the pilot scheme the group divided into three, each with magnetic boards and 'MagNotes'. Each group tackled the three questions. My colleague and I circulated, encouraged and contributed occasionally. As described previously, we clustered the responses and titled the clusters, grouping everyone's work on one large board.

What follows is a broad summary.

☐ The project was necessary and mutually enriching. *Parrains* shared values and vision. It was awareness raising and high-lighted staff and student needs.

☐ There was a lack of recognition by students which was hurtful to some *parrains*. There was too much formality in the first contact with students. Meetings between *parrains* were not scheduled far enough in advance.

☐ *Parrainage* needed to become the heart of EDHEC pedagogy and a focal point within the school. The project needed extend-ing to the entire EDHEC group of schools, it should be inte-grated and understood by all. The present *parrains* needed training and others bringing in. Hearing about other's first-hand experience was considered useful.

The least expected part of our exchange and review was the openness of the group and the level of trust. It was the first time I had been at a meeting where individuals expressed their real concern for the project and what some felt was a lack of success in meeting objectives.

Some contributions:

I would like us to assure that our expectations of the one-to-one relationship are the same as the students'. (*This comment came as a result of students not returning a second time.*)

I would like to find a way to free myself up to have time for students, outside of school and the usual teacher/pupil relationship. (*It was felt that changing environment with its habitual connotations would be more conducive to dialogue.*)

I would like to stop being afraid of being 'unprofessional'; to be able to say 'I can't answer you' and recommend the student goes to see an expert. (*In the French business school tradition, the teacher feels obliged to have the answer. It is almost counter-cultural to use a counselling mode in drawing out the learner's own wisdom and perception. Suggesting a student goes to an expert might be inter-preted as lack of professionalism, and thus of skill, on the part of the* **parrain**.)

I hope to lift the barriers between the student and myself as well as accept that barriers exist. (*We were talking about the difficulty of changing one's attitude.*)

I want to do what I feel is needed without feeling I am being judged. (*There is sometimes a tendency to be in awe of the* **élite**. *Some* **parrains** *felt they were unable to step out of their function within the school*).

I need to learn to listen with more freedom, without being caught up by my own worries.

We had not reached our original objectives

It also became clear that we had not met the objectives in relation to developing competencies, progressing towards clarity in students' career projects and in having a support group that had time for meeting with *parrains*.

It seemed, however, that in the process of defining and working towards our shared objectives we had started to learn. Initially many of us believed we knew how to mentor. The breakthrough was that we began to see it was not so obvious.

Prior to this development, I had not seen that our pilot project could have taken us further than we had hoped when setting ourselves goals. We had made a qualitative change in attitude.

Reviewing with students

During small group workshops, as part of skill and competency orientation, I asked students to work on the question: 'What competencies are needed in order to manage others?'

Figure 2 shows one group's response. This view was not unusual but what is especially interesting is the boxed area sub-titled 'Techniques for Management'. This is the only area students expected to develop at EDHEC.

The purpose of the exercise was to discuss how other areas could be developed, what help was needed and how to get that help.

Towards the end of the session we discussed *parrainage*. Students responses fell into four categories:

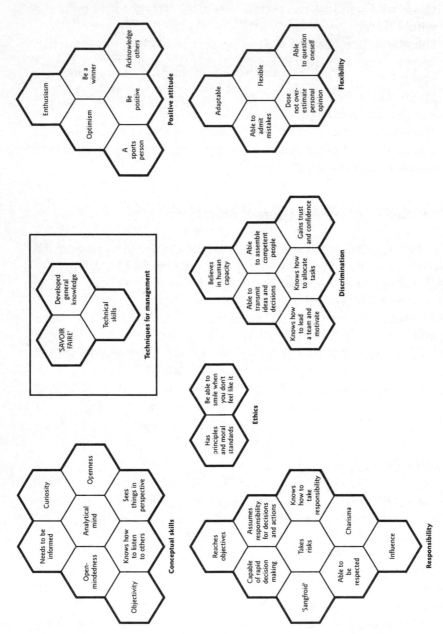

Figure 2 *What competencies are needed in order to manage others?*

1. those who had lost the initial letter, then forgotten about the whole thing
2. those who had been to see their *parrain* and had not returned because they felt they had nothing specific they wanted to talk about
3. those who considered *parrains* should be teaching staff and not from administration
4. those who had gained from getting to know their *parrain*, had learnt about themselves, and considered it a vital contribution to their three years at EDHEC.

Presenting our conclusions to colleagues and Dean

At an end of year meeting we reported on our ARC project on 'mentoring'. We gave the feedback from our final review with *parrains* who suggested *parrainage* becomes central to our pedagogy and integrated into the learning relationship between teachers and students.

It seemed that there was a strategic position to take as the newly developed programme required teaching staff to adopt new roles.

A potential conflict of roles and projects

The new school programme included a module called *Mise en Relation avec l'Entreprise* (MRE) (Practical Exploration of an Organization).

In this five-month module, a tutor was to supervise a small group in their discovery of how a given company functions. The 'tutor' role was to be added to permanent teaching staff responsibilities. For students the module would be compulsory, evaluated in terms of active participation, final written report and group presentation.

To those of us immediately concerned with our pilot project, it was clear that neither the new first-year students nor the staff would cope with both *parrainage* and project tutoring within a complex new programme.

The situation of potential conflict of roles could, however, also have been seen as an opportunity. MRE tutors could be considered as potential mentors in a one-to-one relationship with each student from their group, once their task-oriented function was complete.

If we were to 'accompany' learning then a new sensitivity was needed. Those who had taken part in *parrainage* saw the difference between teaching and this new relationship between the learner and guide.

I attempted to persuade the school Dean and programme director that:

☐ we saw this change of programme as an opportunity to have mentoring central to our role as teachers

☐ those who were to be the new project tutors become mentors

☐ we should enter a period of training in order to be ready to open the new academic year with personal tutoring for all first-year students as a support to the new academic programme.

My request was refused; not because the Dean was unfavourably inclined, but because programme directors were not ready to take on such a radical change. Department heads were even less keen. Those launching MRE saw that my long-term objective was sound, but didn't want to confuse the project tutor role or jeopardize the new programme.

It was July 1994. The academic year had ended. A new programme for the school had been launched. Mentoring through personal tutoring was not included.

Rejection prompted further reflection

For the first time I questioned my capacity for moving the project on to what we had defined as the next stage. It was also the first time that I questioned whether my Anglo-Saxon education and training experience could serve what I believed to be the essential core of our school's pedagogy.

We could not go backwards and I could see no way forward.

During the summer I reflected on the project that seemed to me so fundamentally important, and especially relevant in preparing for management in such an unpredictable period.

Management in France (Barsoux and Lawrence 1990), is fairly revealing of the French Business School tradition. For example: 'Anglo-Saxons' workplace familiarity is shied away from by the French; they do not believe that openness in professional business relations makes sound business sense' … 'France prefers control and command to intuition and openness'.

Referring to in-house training, the authors say 'learning is considered a potentially embarrassing situation – *on se demasque* (we unmask); to mix levels would be to risk erecting psychological barriers to communication'.

Status had not influenced the contributions made to *parrainage*. Everyone's contribution was essential to the work we did. It was not my cultural difference that was inhibiting the project. However, there is a difference between imposing one's will and allowing the situation to reveal its own need and process for achieving the goal.

I reflected on the vulnerability of the hermit crab as he leaves one shell in search of a new one. Like the hermit crab, I needed to find my new shell. It took from June till October to do so.

A new orientation for personal tutoring

In September 1994 I was to present a review of the pilot year of the ARC project together with proposals for 1994/95 to the executive committee.

Where I had jumped several guns in rushing a proposal in June, here I had discussed a possible development with those most concerned with programme development. My proposal had the backing of the head of studies and his immediate team. My search and discussions led to the model shown in Figure 3 which I presented to the executive committee.

We have a three-year programme at EDHEC represented by the four arrows:

> Academic programme
> Work experience
> Career information
> Associations

These arrows are the means by which we target a student to his or her *professional project* (career objectives).

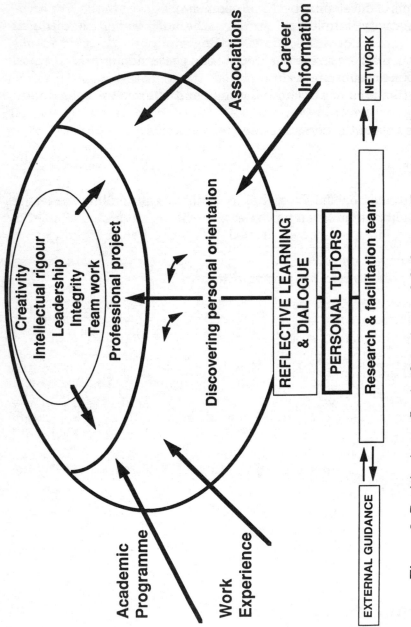

Figure 3 *Positioning reflective learning and dialogue with a personal tutor within a pedagogical framework*

In *parrainage* we focused on the heart of the professional project in terms of developing personal competencies within the five areas of: creativity, intellectual rigour, leadership, integrity and team work.

Without these five areas a student's professional project would be lacking in substance. However, our traditional school programme lacks this area of personal development or focus on behavioural skills.

The role of the personal tutor (or mentor) is:

☐ to enter a one-to-one relationship with the student (the learner)

☐ Through dialogue, to help the student reflect on impacts of the traditional programme, or on experience

☐ To draw out significant learning which will help the learner to learn, set objectives, review progress and further action plans in order to maximize potential.

Before defining a professional project, a student will need to be aware of a broader horizon, termed discovering personal orientation in the model, which ensures that a chosen profession is in harmony with individual talents, aspirations and vocation. This orientation needs to start early enough to ensure that development does not focus solely on the academic or subject specific. While the associations are not part of the academic programme, learning from this area is neglected or overlooked as a means of personal development.

In this model, and with a different understanding of our role as pedagogues, personal tutors come from the school's teaching staff. However we do not know how to tutor in this way, believing personal development to be obvious. We cannot personally tutor (or mentor) without having ourselves been mentored.

The research and facilitation team is there to guide and support the personal tutors by entering into a similar relationship with them, as they will have with students.

The research and development team will, in turn, need support and guidance from their mentor – their external guide. They will also need to learn through networking, research and exchange.

The executive committee agreed to a seminar

I presented our model to the executive committee in October 1994 and asked them to participate in the seminar 'Discovering Personal Orientation', to be facilitated by Jean Motte. Before opening it to students, I suggested evaluating it ourselves. We would not be evaluating intellectually, we would have experienced an event and would have a common language for discussing how we could help students review their learning and base their professional project on their unique talents.

The first seminar was to be for 15 staff – preferably those with direct responsibility for decisions and student programmes. If this test seminar was considered valuable, it could be offered to all staff and then to students. Tutors in the MRE would be consulted before extending their role. Mentoring would remain a matter of personal choice.

The executive committee agreed to a test seminar. After the first seminar and review that followed, decisions would be taken regarding further staff training and whether the seminar was to be integrated into the first-year programme.

Meeting with parrains

Although we had the go-ahead for one seminar and had given ourselves a year to integrate mentoring or personal tutoring within the programme, we still had our *parrainage* project to develop with students who were then in their second year.

We met with the group of *parrains* to share the developments based on our review in May, to share the model as an overview of our joint understanding and to present the seminar proposal. Those who wished to take part in the first seminar were priority participants.

We agreed to personally contact our respective *filleuls* and maintain the relationship. Some *parrains* asked to join the Research and Development Team.

Preparing for the seminar

At the beginning of November, we had 15 participants for our first seminar in mid-November. We had sufficient response to have a second seminar. Some had voiced their disappointment that we had neither mentoring nor a privileged relationship with our new first-year students.

To some, it seemed inevitable that a form of mentoring would follow. Others voiced their surprise at how much progress had been made; what had happened in that year was astonishing. Some referred to the change we were nurturing as a revolution.

Reflections on the project

The chapter has described the rejections and breakthroughs in launching mentoring at a business school in France. I believe the learning is relevant to anyone striving to complement programmes that focus solely on academic excellence.

☐ There is an art in navigating progress, ie in the passionate striving for what one believes in, accepting rejection and being guided by the situation itself. Rejections and contradictions are prerequisites to creative progress.

☐ However vital or personally committed one is to a project, engaging others' active involvement is essential and should be given the time it needs.

☐ Time spent on developing shared vision and objectives is invaluable. Reaching initial objectives is secondary. At a recent meeting a member of staff said, 'There is no conflict between our group's vision of *parrainage* as a complement to subject specific teaching and the school council's mission statement. However, I don't believe they (members of the council) understand the depth of what is at stake.'

☐ She was saying that there was a gap between the mission statement and the real shift of attitude needed by all who form the school's staff. The group of *parrains* understood that they were building a new school culture and a different awareness of their role as teachers for management.

☐ Launching mentoring in the form of *parrainage* and developing the 'soft skills' is counter-cultural because of the nature and tradition of business schools in France and reinforced by the high-power distance (Hofstede 1991).

It remains an on-going challenge but mentoring and behavioural skill development are possible if designed to respond to need and 'mentored in', not imposed. It is neither a matter of grafting on a developmental method from another tradition, nor rejecting others' understanding and discovery.

From the remarks made both by *parrains* and students, I have learned that one of the basic difficulties of *parrainage* or mentoring for us was the first stage of the relationship between mentor and student. Often, neither knew how to get started or what was needed. The student felt awkward, not having a particular problem or issue to discuss. The *parrain* was sometimes unable to get beyond 'chat'.

Apart from having an objective in mentoring, a catalyst is needed as an initial focus for the exchange between mentor and learner. This 'catalyst' could be the BEI (Behavioural Event Interview), referred to earlier, or it could be a seminar that focuses on the students' vocational orientation. The catalyst could likewise be a project such as MRE (Practical Exploration of an Organization).

Our present project is the new seminar. Its purpose is to broaden students' awareness of learning and personal discovery. For the school staff, it is to experience reflective learning and the role of facilitator within the learning process. Figure 4 explains how we propose developing the project further.

It seems the hermit crab has a new shell. MRE has started and I am one of the project tutors. During our first group meeting we discussed the aims and objectives of the project, what was expected and how personal learning was central to the project. One of my students said, 'I think this project is the best thing that has happened at EDHEC. This group is like what they have at Cambridge. I have always wanted to have a tutor'.

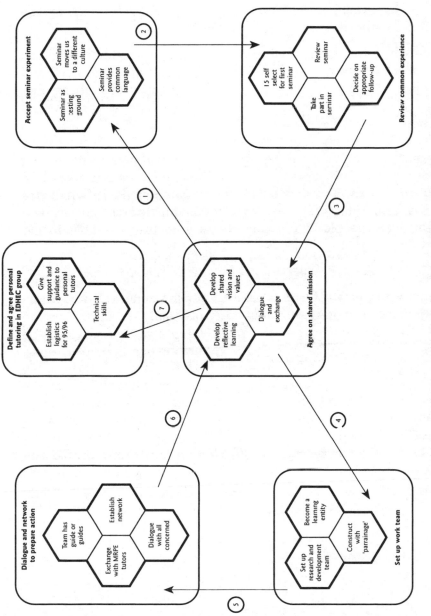

Figure 4 *What is the next phase of personal tutoring at EDHEC?*

The same group set themselves three guiding principals for their MRE project:

☐   to be humble

☐   to be dynamic

☐   to be curious.

What more could be asked for at a first meeting, and what better preparation for mentoring?

Discussion

Cultural issues. These must be taken into consideration at the project design stage: both organizational and national culture have an impact on people's willingness to enter formative relationships.

Training and education. An area that has a crucial importance in clarifying roles and expectations for mentors and learners.

Support for pairs. This is crucial in getting relationships off the ground and managing the mentoring process.

Flexibility. It is essential that the project team is capable of re-thinking and re-grouping in the face of disappointment to carry the scheme through.

References

Barsoux, J and Lawrence, P (1990) *Management in France*, Cassell, London.

Hofstede, G (1991) *Cultures and Organizations: Software of the Mind*, McGraw-Hill, Maidenhead.

4. MAKING MENTORING WORK WITH TRAVEL COUNSELLORS

Linda Holbeche, Roffey Park Management Institute

I imagine that many of us have experienced various forms of mentoring, or may indeed be mentors to other people. In my own experience, being mentored informally by friends has provided an invaluable opportunity to think through my ideas about matters of importance. Acting as a mentor to someone else has been a key developmental experience.

What I am going to describe here is a more formal and conscious form of mentoring, an example of a mentoring scheme that I introduced in my last company for whom I was management development manager in the UK. The mentoring scheme was intended to provide support to people who were taking part in a major development programme.

I am going to outline some of the features of that programme, explain why we thought that a formal mentoring scheme was essential and describe what we did to select and train mentors. I am also going to look at some of the benefits and potential pitfalls of such schemes. I will also be touching on a couple of other aspects of mentoring that are related to the formal mentoring scheme, which are being used successfully in a number of organizations with whom I have worked.

In 1994 I began to research the complex question of career development in flatter structures. The first stage of the research highlighted many of the issues facing employees and organizations when structures are delayered. Typical of these issues is the acute lack of support for many employees whose roles may have changed along with the organization structure.

In the current stage of research, which is establishing case studies of good practice, I am all the more convinced of the value of mentoring as a means of providing developmental support. As well as mentoring by senior people, peer mentoring and self-managed learning are also becoming increasingly relevant as organizations continue to change their structures and increase their demands on employees.

Why the Travel Development Programme?

My last employer was a major organization in the financial services, which also had, as an important part of its portfolio, a travel business dealing in business travel in particular. Like many others, this organization experienced commercial ups and downs during the recession. In order to meet some of the economic challenges, it restructured its operations over three years, removing several management layers.

This in turn created human resource challenges. In the travel business generally there is a shortage of skilled travel counsellors, who, knowing their own worth, tend to hop from organization to organization increasing their skills, knowledge, pay and promotion prospects with each move. By removing layers of management, my last employer was reducing promotion prospects for key personnel. There was a distinct likelihood that retention would become a big problem.

The introduction of a long-term development programme was seen as part of the solution since none of our competitors offered development on such a scale. The aim of the programme was to help employees develop the skills they would need as future managers in line with the way the business was changing. It is true to say that the Travel Development Programme was instigated by the business and designed to meet a specific business need.

Our beliefs about what would be required in managers of the future were based, among other things, on extensive interviews with managers at all levels. These beliefs were then converted into competencies.

In the future organization, heads of business believe that managers will be required to work on the basis of providing appropriate support to their teams rather than taking the approach of command and control. Travel operations will need to be much more customer-focused and offer customers a wider range of tailored products. This in turn will require personnel to understand how businesses operate generally, and this organization in particular.

An alternative form of career development?

The programme was designed to last a minimum of 18 months. Candidates for the programme were considered by the business to be too valuable to lose in the short term. In some cases, employees were already known to be looking for other jobs. Conventionally, a development programme such as this could be perceived as a fast-track programme, but with flatter structures, a fast-track to where?

The philosophy underpinning the programme was that offering people opportunities to develop their skills and experience may provide a viable alternative to the conventional 'onwards and upwards' offered within traditional hierarchical structures. It was therefore extremely important that we managed people's expectations about the programme through consistent messages about the pupose and likely outcomes of the programme.

What does the Travel Development Programme consist of?

The TDP consists of a team-based strategic project sponsored by business heads and a number of training modules related to the competencies, eg greater business awareness. The programme began with a development centre, which served as a benchmark for competencies. The data from the development centre was owned by the participants and formed the basis of a development plan, which was worked out with their mentors and line managers.

The training modules were to be targeted to the participants' areas of competency that were in greatest need of development. We wanted participants to start to take responsibility for managing their own learning, and deliberately left some of the content areas open so that participants could negotiate for specific training or development to support their needs. However, we saw that training modules were only one vehicle for learning and competency development.

Why mentoring?

We saw that there was an irony in providing participants with mentors, almost whether they wanted one or not, as part of a move towards helping them become self-sufficient in development terms.

On the agenda also was the helping of some of our more senior managers, who would be acting as mentors, to become conversant with the skills, knowledge and understanding which we felt future managers would need. We saw that providing mentors allowed the development programme to supply development for both participants and mentors.

The role of mentors

Primarily the mentor's role in the programme was to support and challenge the participant. Each participant would meet with his or her mentor on a monthly basis, between modules. In the first place, mentors were to help participants to review their learning, prepare objectives for forthcoming modules and provide opportunities for broadening their exposure to the business as a whole.

We were conscious of the dangers of 'corporate amnesia' and wanted mentors to be able to spread knowledge and understanding of the company based on their experience, but at the same time we wanted mentors to focus on helping participants build the new skills and understanding required as the business moves forward.

Mentors were also intended to help participants put their current learning into a longer-term context. Participants were likely to discuss career aspirations, competency development and project issues with mentors, whereas current performance issues and development within the current role were the province of the participant's manager. As you can imagine, this was a potential pitfall area.

Who were the mentors?

We invited people to be mentors if we thought that they already had an active interest in development – their own or that of others. This was based on recommendations from business heads, contacts through the training department, etc. We called on managers from not only the travel business but also from sister businesses within the overall organization. We saw mentors as having an active role in some of the modules and wanted them to be able to share good practice from across the businesses.

We were keen to have broadly equal numbers of women and men mentors as we saw this as an opportunity to break stereotypes of what is needed to be a successful manager. We wanted to ensure that mentors were not so senior that they would not easily relate to participants' jobs, but we did have several directors who became mentors.

Preparing for implementation

The TDP began in May 1993. Before the start of the programme, an enormous amount of preparation needed to take place to ensure successful implementation. One of the key elements was that of selection, of both participants and mentors. We also had to decide whether training would be required for mentors, and if so, what form of training. The participants were nominated for the programme by their line managers who had to convince a selection panel of senior managers that their candidate fulfilled the strict criteria.

We decided that we would select mentors according to the criteria I have already outlined, rather than simply looking for volunteers, and that we would train them because we felt that their role would be sufficiently specific to warrant training.

Training mentors

Training for mentors took place just before the official start of the programme. It consisted of a one-day event, covering items such as:

☐ respective roles of learner, line manager and mentor

☐ skills of mentoring

☐ typical mentoring situations

☐ ground rules for mentoring

☐ benefits to the learner, the mentor, the organization

☐ mentoring skills practice

☐ the life cycle of the mentoring relationship.

What was particularly striking was the need expressed by mentors for factual information about the Travel Development Programme and what their role was to be. I was surprised by this since I had supplied them with a detailed written guide about the programme and their role. What I had not taken into account was that few of them would have read it. I had underestimated the need for reassurance and clarity about what can be a fairly organic process. The concerns of the mentors centred on the artificiality of the relationship, and potential overlap between their role and that of the line manager.

This initial training was supplemented throughout the next 18 months with quarterly programme reviews, which allowed training and development professionals to continue to offer relevant training to mentors according to their needs and the phase of the programme. Some mentors received help with career counselling, for example. Interestingly, some (senior) managers who had expressed doubts about the value of skills practice in the initial training became avid supporters of skills practice once the programme was under way.

One piece of learning that grew in importance as the programme began was the need to consult people about the form of communication that they found most helpful. Although this resulted in information being 'drip-fed' throughout the programme in a variety of forms; whole text, bullet points, on paper or by E-mail, the extra effort resulted in mentors and others keeping abreast of each stage in the programme.

Another point of learning was the debate over terms to be used to describe the different players in the mentoring relationship. In my written information, I referred variously to the 'follower' or 'mentee' of the 'mentor'. Mentors took strong exception to the term 'follower', seeing it as a patronizing term. We also discussed the term 'learner', but dismissed that as it seemed to imply that no-one else had anything to learn. We eventually settled for the term 'participant' as a neutral compromise.

Criteria for matching mentors and participants

There were 25 participants in the first TDP. We set ourselves the task of matching participants and mentors, believing that we could give ourselves an administrative and political headache if we gave all concerned a free choice. We matched mentors and participants on the basis of two main criteria:

☐ *geography*: we wanted to make it possible for participants and mentors to meet, so we tried to ensure that they were within easy travelling distance of each other

☐ *scope*: we hoped to offer participants a mentor from a different part of the business who could offer a different perspective on the business. In some cases, the mentor was from a different business altogether.

We prepared dossiers on both mentors and participants. First we sent the dossier of the suggested participant to the mentor to ensure that they had no strong objection to the match. We then repeated the process with the participants, allowing both parties a cooling-off period before the programme got under way. We had to arrange a couple of swaps where the partipant or mentor raised objections.

The role of training and development professionals

Undoubtably the most labour-intensive part of the process was the period of consultation and preparation leading up to the start of the programme and the early stages of implementation. Our role was primarily that of co-ordinator, ensuring that everybody had the information needed to play their respective parts in the programme.

Initially we were proactive in requesting and disseminating information, but later we put systems in place which ensured that we were prompted to act when need be. By then, we were comfortable in the knowledge that people had been 'trained' to communicate necessary information to each other. We were anxious to respect the confidentiality of the mentoring relationship, and yet the more participants seemed to be benefiting from the mentoring relationship, the more their line managers wanted to be kept informed of their progress.

Sometimes we had sensitive issues to address, such as helping one or two participants who had over-protective or eventually incompatible mentors. There was a surprising turnover among mentors with several leaving the company for positions of higher responsibility elsewhere. This was the only reason for mentors wishing to relinquish the role. As time moved on, we had a list of would-be mentors waiting for the opportunity to act as mentor. They were kept informed and involved in the programme so that they would be in tune with events should they be called upon.

As training and development professionals we had to ensure that we were providing mentors and participants with the support they needed. Learning from our early mistakes of drowning people in information, we gradually engaged both mentors and participants in drawing up suggestions on how to develop each of the competency areas. These were then converted into resource guides, which looked at each competency from either the mentoring or the self-development angle.

The key to the success of these resources was their timing – only introduced when the need for them was felt, and with the involvement of all concerned in drawing them up. Needless to say, the same information was then produced in a variety of formats, including neat loose-leaf pages that were able to fit participants' time management systems.

We also had to ensure that senior sponsors remained committed and involved in the programme, which we did in a variety of ways both formal and informal. This entailed ensuring sufficient visibility for the programme internally and externally.

In the earliest part of the programme following the development centre, participants and mentors needed most support from the training and development group. I was the manager and overall coordinator of the programme with the business, and I was supported by a trainer who acted as a liaison point for participants.

Implementation

We encouraged mentors and participants to meet with the participants' line managers in order to establish some ground rules for the relationship from the outset. These ground rules and the separate responsibilities of all three parties were laid out in a contract that established the parameters of the respective relationships.

As the programme developed, the need for communication increased in order to maintain the momentum and understanding of all concerned about what they needed to do next as they moved to a different phase in the programme. There is no doubt that mentors took their responsibilities extremely seriously. Some were upset if the participant had not contacted them in the early days of the programme.

This presented trainers and mentors with a nice dilemma: should participants be free not to use the services of a mentor if they so desired and were we flying in the face of the spirit of self-development by insisting that they should? However, whether through peer pressure or the evident benefits some participants were deriving from the mentoring relationship, all participants eventually made contact with their mentors and used the relationship as a resource to further their own development.

Mentors continued to have a shaping role in the development of the programme itself, as they were able to feed back their concerns or recommendations at each stage in the quarterly reviews. Indeed, the benefits of mentoring seemed to generate a couple of other support activities that are very similar to the work developed at Roffey Park. Participants in particular took to working very closely in project teams, and derived a lot of benefit from the support of their peer group.

At Roffey Park, the idea has been refined to a deliberate form of peer mentoring, a type of support that seems very appropriate to flatter organization structures in which it is likely that there will be fewer managers to become mentors for others. It involves training pairs or groups of peers, including those engaged in customer-supplier relationships, in some basic counselling skills and deliberate contracting based on feedback. The results seem to indicate mutual benefits from the career strategizing and information-sharing that takes place. Organizations where peer mentoring has been introduced report improved teamwork and morale, since peers are able to supply a level of confirmation and emotional support often lacking in times of change.

Another outcome of the mentoring programme is that some mentors have enjoyed helping other people develop but have become hungry to focus on their own development. This has led to the formation of informal learning groups, meeting together to pursue their own learning goals. At Roffey Park this approach is reflected in self-managed learning, in which adults working in learning sets with a set adviser pursue their individual learning outcomes with the support and challenge of their set. Increasingly organizations are recognizing the value of self-managed learning and some are encouraging participants to consider attending 'set' meetings as a business priority.

This seems to be such a powerful form of learning that 'sets' persist over time, even though circumstances change. As one member of a year-old set put it, 'self-managed learning is Roffey's best kept secret'. Fortunately the approach is not so secret, and it has been successfully introduced into a number of client companies with remarkable results.

Potential pitfalls

Of course, things were not all plain sailing. A key pitfall area to be avoided was confusion over respective roles. We learned that greater clarity at the beginning of the programme, and allowing line managers to express any misgivings, are important. Clearly if a mentoring relationship interferes with, or usurps the role of, the manager, problems are likely to ensue. We found the three-way meeting, the establishing of ground rules and a formal contract between all parties about what it was appropriate for mentoring to cover, allayed many initial doubts.

Another potentially sensitive area is the matching of mentors and participants. I hoped to provide women participants with women mentors, believing that this would be a good way to provide role models who may have experienced similar challenges. When I made this suggestion, it was heavily rejected by both participants and mentors. Some male mentors interpreted my intention as insulting to them, while many women considered my suggestion patronizing. Some organizations with which I am currently working, however, are using this gender match to accelerate the progression of women to more senior positions. The area is open to much debate!

Since the role of mentor calls on many skills and a flexible approach, we found that some mentors became progressively ineffective in the eyes of participants. They were happy in the role of sage dispensing advice, but were not necessarily encouraging participants to find their own solutions. We also had one or two examples of mentors encouraging dependency in the participants and actually taking over arrangements for the participants' development.

When this became apparent, we saw our responsibility in training and development as not rescuing the participants but helping them to develop sufficient assertiveness to express their needs and give feedback on how they were being met. Gradually these problems eased through the ongoing training opportunities that the mentors' quarterly reviews gave us, and because of the requirement we placed on both mentors and participants to give each other feedback in a structured way. We had to replace only one mentor who remained impervious to what was required.

Benefits to participants

Such was the value of the mentoring relationship that several participants whose mentor left the company insisted on having a replacement mentor. Some, indeed, maintained a mentoring relationship with their departed mentor. What participants particularly appreciated was having someone, who was not their immediate line manager, to talk to about career and other matters. In some cases they considered their mentor a role model. Others reported on how much they had learned about their own learning preferences, in contrast to their mentor's style. Almost all have volunteered to be mentors in their turn.

Benefits to mentors

Most mentors found the role extremely satisfying, since they valued being able to assist someone else in their development. As mentors, they were able to pick up new ideas and have an active part in shaping the future management cadre of the organization. Inevitably the process of mentoring involved the giving and receiving of feedback, and some had found the gradual challenging of their views developmental in itself. A key benefit reported by mentors was the development of their own networks and support systems among fellow mentors across the organization.

Benefits to training and development professionals

Despite the effort involved, seeing the mentoring programme develop its own momentum, visibly adding value to those concerned, made the effort worthwhile. Training is often seen as a cost to businesses, yet this mentoring-based programme, sponsored by senior management, was a visible example of the importance of investing in developing staff. The retention rates alone made the investment worthwhile, and the improved morale of people in managerial positions has a knock-on effect elsewhere in the business. As training and development professionals, it is pleasant to be associated with a programme that is seen to be successful by any standards.

Benefits to the organization

Mentoring provided the organization with multiple benefits; not only were participants being developed in line with the business's longer-term strategy, but so were a more senior team of managers, thus ensuring a sufficient mass to start the process of culture change. Indeed, some of these successful managers may have been in danger of plateauing. Their recharged interest in development ensured that this would not happen.

This linking of slightly more senior experience with the enthusiasm and potential of participants has ensured that communication channels have been established across line or matrix boundaries. This in turn has reinforced the development of a team culture, a vital ingredient in an organization aspiring to total quality. In addition, through the mentoring programme, the visibility of individuals has been raised and a number of lateral moves have ensured that the organization is benefiting from the enhanced skills of participants.

The key objective of the programme, ie retention of key employees, seems to have been achieved, with remarkably little turnover of staff among the participant group. Indeed, of the original 25, only one has left, for personal reasons. From the earliest days of the programme, participants were reporting envy expressed by competitors' employees, met through their own networks. If anything, the programme was a key part of the enhanced reputation of the organization as an employer in the marketplace, thus making it attractive to potential entrants.

Conclusion

The evidence of the success of the mentoring programme is that there are now as many volunteer mentors as there are would-be participants. The momentum that has built up around the programme has meant that the second cohort began only nine months into the first programme, and is meeting with similar success. Several of the original mentors are taking their ongoing development seriously and in some cases are following MBA or professional development programmes. Certainly the process of mentoring seems to have fostered an ethic of continuous improvement.

So mentoring and self-development, rather than being paradoxical, seem to have worked hand-in-hand. As Clutterbuck and Devine (1987) put it:

> The essence of mentoring is closely allied to self-development. Both approaches have the ultimate aim of helping an individual grow as a person and take responsibility for his or her own development. If the two ... approaches become more widespread, self-development and mentoring promise to be exciting partners.

Discussion

Terms. It is difficult to find the right term for the person mentored. We use 'learner', though various cases prefer 'mentee' or 'participant.'

Line manager involvement. Tensions and role conflict need to be addressed.

Voluntary or compulsory? The self-managed emphasis of this scheme led to allowing take-up to be voluntary.

Gender. In this case cross gender mentoring was not seen as problematic.

Reference

Clutterbuck, D and Devine, M (eds) (1987) *Businesswoman*, Macmillan, London.

5. POSITIVE ACTION LEADERSHIP SPONSOR SCHEME AT LEWISHAM COUNCIL

Mary Evans, Management Development Consultant

Lewisham Council has been operating a structured mentoring scheme for Black staff, entitled positive action leadership sponsor scheme, for just over two years. It is managed corporately within the personnel and administration division by the management development unit and encourages both Black and White sponsors in an attempt to overcome the marginalization of Black staff's career development and to foster organizational ownership and commitment.

Background

The council has long recognized that the people it employs are its most valuable resource. In 1990, the personnel division commissioned the research and production of a far-reaching and forward-thinking human resource strategy that would enable it to maintain a motivated and competent workforce. Through implementation of this strategy, the organization aims to continue to provide quality services to the community as it approaches and moves into the twenty-first century.

One of the five priority areas highlighted for action in the strategy is positive action to assist the career development of Black employees within the organization. The council's annual workforce survey has continued to show that while the numbers of Black people employed by the council is generally representative of the local community, there is an under-representation of Black people in all management grades, and most particularly in middle and senior management. This under-representation limits Lewisham's capacity to respond proactively to the service demands of a multi-racial customer base. An under-representation of Black managers also means that Lewisham is not using the skills and abilities of the Black people it employs.

All work within the organization is influenced by the following set of core values:

☐   local government is about serving local people

☐   putting services to the public first

☐   aiming for quality

☐   equality of opportunity for all sections of the community and the workforce

☐   valuing people

☐   taking action to be effective and efficient

☐   caring for the environment

The scheme is validated in the council by its orientation to 'valuing people' and 'equal opportunities'.

Development of the scheme

A working party of officers from across the authority met regularly to brainstorm, research and problem-solve the issues around current support provision; the blocks that Black staff face, and the feasibility of various developmental opportunities. The group discovered that although much was being provided already in the field of positive action training, the main provision came in the form of, short courses, away from the workplace, with little relationship between the two. People would be energized and empowered by these courses in the short term, but not only was there concern about their long-term effect, they also served to emphasize the marginalization of Black people in the organization. The courses always received excellent feedback from participants, however, so in order to build upon this provision the external trainers from the programme were consulted and involved in the subsequent development of the scheme.

The other main area of provision was that of Black staff groups/forums, which provided valuable support and networking, but again militated against White managers taking ownership issues. Some research into the provision offered by the neighbouring local authorities found that their best practice was very similar to our current provision. The group concluded that what was needed was a creative system of on-going support and learning, able to address the blocks identified as facing Black managers, such as limited knowledge of 'the way we do things round here', low access to the necessary networks, and limited awareness of political and organizational issues.

We also felt the need to address the perceived management development needs in this area in an indirect fashion. Mentoring, as a process, was discussed, but the name was rejected as the group felt that mentoring involves the ability to fully appreciate and understand the aspirations and pressures of the mentee, and to serve as a role model for them. This implies the need for Black mentors, for which more Black managers would be needed than were available. The scheme was developed based on mentoring as a process, but promoting equal responsibility between Black and White staff and also looking towards addressing managers' development needs around the management of diversity.

Marketing the scheme

The working party was clear that in order for the scheme to be successful in gaining participation and support, it needed to gain credibility as an activity for those with power in the organization. We were also clear that, in striving to become a learning organization, valuable learning can be gained from testing an initiative before its main implementation. We decided therefore to set up a 3-month pilot scheme involving four members of the working party, with influential and organizationally powerful senior managers as sponsors. The pilot was evaluated by interview of all those involved and the benefits found were publicized widely including both the use of the highly accessible council newsletters and that of the organizationally established top-down briefing system. Marketing is also targeted on an ongoing basis to participants on the corporate training courses for Black managers and Black staff wanting to move into management, as it provides complementary and longer-term support for their development.

Learning points from the pilot

There proved to be a fair amount of diversity in the methods of the sponsoring partnerships and the desire of those involved for a structured framework. The implication taken from this for the scheme's management was the need to maintain a balance between the provision of enough structure for the scheme without being too prescriptive and thus stifling the possibilities. In addition, all involved reported difficulties in achieving the time away from other work commitments, and found that their meetings were therefore fairly irregular. Given that those involved with the pilot had a relatively high degree of control over their time, this looked like a potential difficulty, particularly for participants at lower levels in the organization.

The pilot also fulfilled what proved to be a crucial role in our involvement of influential senior managers at the scheme's early stages. As these managers were able to experience and benefit from the scheme themselves, and were genuinely involved in the shaping of the scheme, their ownership of it at this stage, and their willingness to be involved in publicity, was extremely beneficial in the subsequent marketing.

The structure of the scheme

Application and matching process

The management development unit holds a database of managers, who have volunteered to be sponsors on the scheme. Interested Black and ethnic minority employees apply by completing an application form that asks for initial expectations of the scheme, and this is then followed up by a matching interview where employees explore their needs and expectations further and choose a potential sponsor from the information contained on the database. If there is no obvious match, or the sponsee has a specific development need, other managers will be targeted as potential sponsors and approached by the management development unit. The matching process is completed with an introductory interview, at which point an initial commitment is made, although there is no blame or penalty attached if at any stage participants feel that they have benefited all they can from the process.

Guidelines

The process followed by each sponsoring partnership will vary according to the skills and resources of the sponsor and the needs of the sponsee, and this diversity is encouraged. In order to ensure some consistency to aid evaluation of the scheme and to give the reassurance of a structure, a suggested framework and ground rules are discussed at the introductory interview, focusing on the formulation of learning objectives and giving a guide to the necessary time commitment. At all times there is emphasis on the sponsee's ownership of their learning and the setting of realistic goals based on the resources offered by the sponsor, and the energy that they can themselves devote to the exercise. The nature of organizational change at Lewisham has meant that short-term arrangements are more easily accepted and sustained, and therefore the recommended time commitment for the scheme is six months to one year, with at least one meeting a fortnight to maintain the momentum. If a sponsoring partnership reaches its potential before this time, the scheme is flexible enough to allow movement between sponsors, and in some cases this proves necessary to supplement the sponsor's skills and resources. A pack of support materials is given to the participants at this time, including such items as a self-assessment skills checklist for sponsors, a learning beliefs questionnaire for sponsors, reflection and action planning forms, and a SWOT grid.

Training and support

Although initial training was arranged for sponsors, it did not prove to be successful, as the skills needs of the participants were so diverse and their need for details of the scheme itself was more appropriately met by the provision of written information. Sponsees were however much more inclined to meet and learn as a group, and therefore facilitated-support workshops are arranged four times a year, which focus on how the sponsees can maximize the benefits of participating in the scheme. All sponsors and sponsees can also draw support on an individual or partnership basis from the management development unit.

Link with line manager

The council has recently introduced, as part of the organizational change process, an employee development scheme that is a structured mechanism for the setting of individual work objectives within organizational objectives. The scheme aims to include an analysis of training needs and planning for appropriate development opportunities, in twice-yearly meetings between employees and their manager. The scheme stresses the importance of creativity and relevance in the choice of development options rather than the over-use of the traditional form of training course. As an innovative means of clarifying and addressing Black staff's development needs the sponsor scheme was introduced at an opportune time to provide a tool for managers in this process. Feedback to managers throughout the process, in particular in terms of objectives set and actions planned, is crucial. The benefit of this to the Black staff involved is a higher level of commitment to the process from the manager and therefore a greater inclination to allow staff the opportunity to engage in developmental activities away from the workplace.

Results

Evaluation of the scheme is partially through an annual review involving feedback by questionnaires, and by interviews, where participants are asked about their experiences on the scheme. Measurement of the scheme's effectiveness in addressing the organizational need for greater representation of Black managers is a longer-term exercise. It will always be difficult to draw a direct link between development activities and career advancement. Career tracking of all Black staff who have been sponsored on the scheme is, however, carried out to provide preliminary data.

The findings of the review undertaken in July/August 1994 were as follows:

☐ all currently involved expressed satisfaction with the scheme and the majority of sponsees felt it would help their career progression

☐ twenty-four per cent of Black staff who had been sponsored on the scheme at some time had achieved higher-graded posts; 30 per cent of these were outside the organization

☐ a further 10 per cent had undertaken secondments or other long-term developmental activities within the organization as a direct result of their participation.

Sponsees currently involved in the scheme identified the following benefits to themselves:

- [ ] insights into other parts of the organization, their methods of working and their culture

- [ ] experience of new activities

- [ ] self analysis/skills audits

- [ ] development of self-confidence

- [ ] development of communication skills and other personal competencies

- [ ] networking with other sponsees

- [ ] development of problem-solving ability and the use of others as a sounding board

- [ ] personal support.

Current sponsors identified the following benefits to themselves:

- [ ] practice at coaching, counselling and career counselling

- [ ] feedback on skill

- [ ] learning about a Black woman's perspective on life and work

- [ ] learning about different areas of work and others' experiences

- [ ] the discipline of giving dedicated, regular time

- [ ] stimulating ideas, interesting discussion, exchanging skills

- [ ] helpful to be in touch with someone 'at the sharp end'.

Sponsors also identified the following as benefits to the organization:

- [ ] interdepartmental awareness

- [ ] increased commitment to the organization

- [ ] improvements in management practice

- [ ] increase in service performance

- [ ] the practical implementation of the core values

☐   increased employee flexibility and ability to respond to change

☐   greater awareness of cultural differences

☐   greater ability to produce 'home grown' managers.

In March 1993, soon after the scheme's introduction, we were given a SOCPO (Society of Chief Personnel Officers) Award for innovation in local government personnel practice.

Conclusions

The scheme has been in full operation since December 1992 and has so far seen 50 partnerships on a rolling basis. It continues to be supported by senior managers and council members and appears on review to be a worthwhile and effective method of facilitating the career development of Black staff.

The scheme is very strongly and deliberately based on organizational objectives. These objectives are to increase the representation of Black staff in middle and senior management positions through addressing both the development needs of Black staff in the organization and also those of White managers in managing a multi-racial workforce.

We recognize that evaluation of the scheme against these organizational objectives will be difficult and will need to be on a long-term basis. This organizational validation for individual development has, however, proved extremely beneficial in ensuring the availability of the necessary resources. The cost of the scheme has been minimal in financial terms (only for marketing and support groups) but considerable in terms of staff and manager time.

Discussion

Senior management involvement. The participation of influential senior managers, acting as role models for sponsors and breaking down the old hierarchical relationships, has been crucial for the scheme's success.

Organization culture. The effectiveness of the scheme has also been determined by the culture at Lewisham within which creativity and flexibility at work are increasingly encouraged, where equal opportunities are well established, and where the link between organizational objectives and individual development is clearly drawn.

Piloting. Piloting mentoring schemes is shown to be useful not only in identifying difficulties and suitable approaches, but also in engaging the strong support of senior management.

Link to line manager. The performance management process in the authority is clearly the responsibility of the line manager. The mentoring (or sponsoring) activity remains separate.

Mentor/learner training. In this scheme, mentors seemed reluctant to make use of meeting together to share experience, whereas learners were not. The strong identification between learners (as Black managers) helped them to work.

6. BENEFITS AGENCY STAFF DEVELOPMENT SCHEME

Pam Fricker, Training Operations, Benefits Agency

The idea for a staff development scheme was born out of a workshop held in the area. Participants discussed what opportunities there were within the area, and agreed that a formal scheme would be a way of improving staff development, particularly with the reduction in vertical career opportunities. Mentoring was an important element of the scheme, in that it provided the participants with a sounding board and advisor outside the normal line management structure.

The scheme is not targeted at any one grade, function or 'category', although it is generally intended to assist in development of all grades from junior clerical to middle management.

The scheme is distinct from other training and development programmes in the area in that participants choose specific areas for development that may fall outside normal parameters. Part of the purpose of the scheme is to enable participants to achieve something to which they would not usually have access. In this process, other training and development needs may become apparent, and in personal development, the mentoring through the staff development scheme complements the line manager role.

Marketing and matching

Advertisements were placed in newsletters, and presentations were made at local meetings and at the Area Training Network meeting. In addition, two 'open days' were held, with guest speakers from other staff development schemes (within the BA) sharing their experiences.

The intention was that mentors would be interviewed and selected using criteria such as personal attitude to staff development, experience, and commitment. In fact, interviews were not conducted, as the number of applicants matched exactly the number of mentors required, and all were considered suitable.

Applicants to the scheme were interviewed by the organizers. Criteria for selection were again principally around the candidate's attitude to development, and his or her commitment and enthusiasm for personal growth.

The scheme operates with two participants to each mentor. The matching was done by the organizers, and decisions on matching were made by considering the base locations and ensuring that the mentor was from a different district wherever possible. Personal knowledge of mentors and candidates was also used in matching personalities.

Guidelines and training

No formal guidelines were issued in the first year, but some recommendations were made in the initial training event for mentors. Guidelines covering how often they should meet their participants, where, when, and so on were discussed, and the mentors considered ground rules for their relationships at that event.

In the first year the only training specifically for the mentors was an initial event of three days. Through the year there were three further events for mentors and participants together, to look at specific training areas identified, though these were not directly related to mentor skills and covered areas such as presentation skills and marketing. Other than that, training in other skills areas identified by the mentors was available from Benefits Agency Training, and other training organizations in the normal way (ie no specific training events for them were arranged).

Support for mentors/mentees

The organizing group are there to support both mentors and participants, particularly in an administrative sense. During the year, the mentors found that they supported each other informally. For the second year, mentors will be 'paired' during the first training event, as a more formal start to networking and supporting each other.

Managing the programme

The mentor and participant agree learning objectives, and review these together.

The organizers manage the programme in terms of administration (organizing events, managing the budget, etc), and in determining the length of the mentoring arrangements.

During the first year of this scheme there were no formal arrangements for measuring the success of the relationships. Two mentors withdrew from the programme, but this was not necessarily due to the relationship with participants.

Reviewing the scheme

The scheme was reviewed through the year at events for mentors, participants and organizers. In addition, the mentors met together to review progress. At the end of the year, the organizers briefed the area management team on how things had gone, and through this secured agreement and funding for the second year. Two open days were held, at which participants and mentors made their portfolios available, showing what had been achieved through the year. Mentors, participants and organizers also spoke about their experiences through the year, and took questions from the audience.

A variety of problems were identified during the review process. Among them:

☐ Not all mentors and participants were able to attend all the workshop events scheduled through the year, because they were often away from the office.

☐ Some fear and suspicion was encountered from colleagues who were not participating in the scheme. This seems to be due partially to a lack of knowledge of what the scheme is about, and a lack of support from peers. The workshop events, being residential, were sometimes viewed rather cynically by those not participating in the scheme.

☐ One of the biggest limitations has been the lack of time for mentors to devote to participants. There are no additional resources to support the mentors for time away from the office while fulfilling their mentoring roles.

Conclusion

The organizers feel that the selection process is very important, and should be based on advertised criteria. There also needs to be a structure for the scheme, and progress should be checked and evaluated during the length of the mentoring relationship. The ratio of one mentor to two participants seems to be effective, but it is felt that no-one could be as effective with more than two participants. Another important contribution that the scheme makes is that it has proved developmental for the mentors as well as for the participants. There has been clear value to the organization.

Discussion

Control. This is an example of a scheme where mentors were consulted about its nature at the start, but after that control of the scheme was retained by the training function, who provided a high level of continuing support for mentors and participants.

Training Support. Continuity, and an opportunity to network and exchange views, seem to be the key contribution that mentors and participants require from the training function. In this case participants and mentors attended the training together, and this has been well received.

Benefits. In this organization, benefits to mentors were seen as a major outcome of the scheme. In a sense, the scheme provided an opportunity to have more senior managers (the mentors) acknowledge their need for training and development under the guise of helping someone else.

7. LET THE ACTIONS MATCH THE WORDS: ENGINEERING UK

Bob Garvey, University of Durham Business School

The aim

The aim of this case study is to examine the key elements of Engineering UK's unsuccessful mentor scheme. It describes an approach to establishing a mentor scheme that was linked to a major development programme and debates the possible causes of failure.

Engineering UK is an actual company but, at its request, all names have been changed.

Background

Engineering UK is part of a multi-national engineering company that operates in a highly competitive, international market.

This competition issue became a major consideration when recently one competitor made a head-on assault on their customer base. Engineering (worldwide) responded by making an appeal to the workforce to meet the challenge of competition. This was largely achieved within a 30-month period and as a result, Engineering (worldwide) held its customer base.

In order to continue this dramatic success, Engineering (worldwide) created a new corporate 'customer led' strategy that senior management hoped would enable them to maintain and develop further the company's world market position.

The communication of this strategy to the world sites seemed to involve a great number of slogans – for example, 'continuous improvement', 'benchmarking', 'learning organisation' 'common approach', 'We're in it for the long haul'. There were also numerous manuals, texts and presentations issued by the parent company. Key staff were expected to implement these dictates. The contents of these directives, while recognizing the need to make operational and structural changes within the organization, also acknowledged the importance of gaining the commitment of the whole workforce.

The new strategy involved dramatic changes that revolved around a review, and subsequent introduction of new production methods and new management approaches.

Internationally, a major training and development programme was established to support the strategy. The programme was aimed at the whole workforce, from senior managers to hourly paid workers, but there was a clear primary focus of attention on first line supervisors and their team members.

At the heart of the development programme the company established a mentor scheme to support the development of participating individuals.

Central to this international programme for all people was the slogan 'the common approach'. This meant that all training inputs, development systems and evaluation processes were underpinned by constant reference to Engineering's (worldwide) objectives.

Through this approach of working to a common agenda, Engineering (worldwide) expected that all sections of the company would develop in the same direction and emerge with a shared philosophy.

Birth of mentoring in the UK

Although in concept the mentor scheme was born out of the development programme, its growth from infancy had much wider expectations.

In introducing mentoring to the UK programme the UK training manager used a similar approach to Kram's (1985) model for achieving a successful mentor scheme. This model is used in this case study as the framework to help to describe the extent of expectations from mentoring at Engineering UK.

The Kram model

Kram identified four stages to developing a mentor scheme.

1. defining the scope of the project
2. diagnosis
3. implementation
4. evaluation.

The scope

The purpose of the Engineering UK scheme was to 'provide the yeast in the bread' for the changes. Mentors were seen by the training manager as having a key role in the success of the programme. Their main function was to help identify opportunities for applying the newly acquired learning from the development programme into the workplace.

Mentors were also asked to discuss career opportunities and to help resolve learning difficulties in a supportive and personal environment. They were not briefed to 'control' events but to act as independent counsellors and guides for their 'clients'. (The term 'client' is discussed later.)

It was also intended that the mentor process should be two-way in that the client needed to influence the mentor's thinking as much as the other way round.

Additionally, the Engineering UK mentor scheme was established to offer ease of induction for new recruits and to provide the opportunity for clients to gain quickly a better understanding of the formal structures of the organization.

And another thing!

The mentor scheme was also expected to address the following:

1. recent redundancies and de-skilling
2. the need for improved individual effectiveness
3. internal cultural change.

Redundancies and de-skilling

Engineering UK has a history of industrial unrest and at the time of this initiative they had just reduced the size of the workforce due to the increased use of high technology. This created the classic fears in the workforce of, 'if we work hard and commission these new machines, we lose our jobs and if we don't lose our jobs, we become de-skilled'. This feeling of a loss of trust and an increase in suspicion for management among those left after the redundancy round was very strong at the time of this new initiative. There was also evidence of resentment among people for the insensitivity of management in making people redundant following the successful drive to head-off competition.

The mentor scheme was expected to help re-build trust between management and the shop floor and address the de-skilling issue by seeking areas of skill development through the mentor process.

The need for greater effectiveness

With fewer people and more technology, the company needed all individuals to be more effective and adaptable at work.

The mentor scheme was expected to help facilitate flexible working and enhance individual performance.

Internal culture change

A heavy command and control culture in Engineering UK was recognized by the training manager and it was his wish that this should change to a leadership culture.

The mentor scheme was placed at the heart of this cultural change and it was envisaged that mentoring would both empower the workforce by giving real authority to both the mentor and the client. It would help to create and maintain the 'continuous improvement' process by creating a new dynamic 'learning culture' in the organization where opportunities for development would be encouraged.

The scope of the mentor scheme was, therefore, very wide and the reliance on the mentor scheme to help 'the bread rise' was great.

The diagnosis

The training manager set about gaining information on the attitudes, skills and knowledge of the potential participants in the mentor scheme in order to help plan the approach to mentoring.

It was discovered that some potential mentors had a poor comprehension of how development impacts on the career progression and personal growth of people. This led to a view held by some potential mentors that people development was secondary and unimportant.

The diagnosis identified that if a potential mentor had no positive personal experience of mentoring he (no female mentors) might be opposed to the scheme.

Some potential mentors were experiencing blockages in their own career progression and therefore were not very keen to help another person.

Another potential difficulty was the deeply embedded culture in the organization. The training manager felt that individuals might not consciously attempt to thwart the culture change but might be driven by a powerful subconscious force based on the notion of 'this is not the way I did it' and 'I did it the hard way and so should you'.

Getting personal

The personal attributes of a mentor were also considered and the training manager identified these as follows:

1. interest
2. supportive
3. position
4. influence
5. security
6. time
7. leadership.

Interest

Mentors needed to have a genuine interest in being a mentor because imposing the role on an unwilling individual could spell disaster for the relationship.

Supportive

Mentors needed to be individuals who supported the changes or at least who had an open mind towards change.

Position

Mentors should be senior to the client but not the clients' direct manager. In some cases, the mentor could be somebody of equal status in the organization but with a greater, wider or different experience.

Influence

The mentor should be somebody of influence within Engineering UK and therefore able to access the various networks of communication and to understand the political make-up of the organization.

Security

Potential mentors needed to be established in their career so that they would avoid seeing the client as a threat to their position. The relationship needed to be one based on mutual respect, trust and a sense of camaraderie.

Time

The mentor needed to be prepared to give time for face-to-face discussions of the issues raised and identified as part of the continuous improvement process.

Leadership

Successful mentors often possess good leadership qualities (Clutterbuck 1992) in that they are able to motivate, listen, support and challenge. So, people with a record of demonstrating leadership qualities could be considered for the mentor role. It was also envisaged that this would help to develop the leadership culture.

Mentor skills were also identified and categorized as follows:

☐ *personal skills*: personal management abilities, ie ability to listen, interpret and comment, ability to manage time

☐ *inter-personal skills*: skills necessary to facilitate good inter-personal relationships, often dependent on attitudes, ie counselling, coaching, challenging, questioning.

The training manager wanted the mentor scheme to be based on a counselling approach. He saw this as the key skill.

Implementation

The first step taken was to select appropriate people to act as mentors. This was done by issuing the character attributes and skill criteria to the various plant managers and asking them to nominate potential mentors, basing their nominations on the criteria. Once this was done, the client selected a mentor of their choice from the resulting list. Each selection was discussed with the line manager, mentor, plant manager and training manager and, where appropriate, agreed. There was no guarantee of agreement, although most selections were accepted. The relationship was then established as a formal one.

The mentor nominees attended a day-and-a-half's training programme to learn the principles of the scheme and to understand their role.

Mentor skills were not addressed as it was assumed that nominee mentors already had the skills necessary to be a mentor by virtue of their experience.

The withering death

According to the training manager, the development programme has been working well but the mentor scheme has had many problems. However, it was reviewed and further training and development needs for mentors were identified. These were particularly in understanding the nature of adult learning, coaching and counselling. In fact, some mentors were clearly confused as to the difference between coaching and counselling.

More time was needed from the human resource development specialists to support the process in order to facilitate greater collaboration between the HRD people, the mentors and their clients. There was a need for more educational inputs in order to address attitudinal resistance to change and there was a need to consider the reward and recognition issues for people fulfilling the mentor role.

They needed a new implementation programme to address the problems. But, despite the care taken to identify these and desire of the training manager to seek solutions, the commitment to mentoring shown by the participants had disappeared. As a result, the mentor scheme soon withered and died.

The post-mortem

The tragedy of this death was that most of the causes were identified by the training manager during the diagnosis phase, but deeply embedded attitudes became the barriers to change.

Hard driving change

Engineering (worldwide) is a highly competitive business that needs to make certain that internal changes happen quickly. There was a conflict here as mentor development cannot be hurried, particularly in a potentially hostile environment (Kram 1985). This driving competitiveness contributed to the macho management attitudes, which are still very evident within Engineering UK. It is likely that these are the main cause of death of the mentoring scheme.

This can be demonstrated in many ways. The international strategy seemed to be formed by the parent company using the Taylorist 'one best way' philosophy and then imposed with the 'we know what that approach is' method. This contrasts strongly with, say, the approach to strategy taken at Rover or Ilford Films. Here the overall framework is decided by senior management but the details of implementation are left to the various working groups within the organization who are empowered to use their expertise to influence and affect the strategy. (See *Managing Performance*, BBC Training, 1994.)

Understanding the importance of culture in the mentor process

A 'macho', 'autocratic' culture undermined the mentoring process. Mentoring is not about giving instructions and advice, which is the natural inclination of autocratic management. Mentoring requires a counselling, supporting, challenging and developmental approach. In an environment of command and control, this would not be the normal behaviour of senior management as it might well be regarded as 'soft' and a 'waste of time'.

The assumption was that potential mentors would have acquired both the understanding and the skills of mentoring simply by being experienced. However, skills are acquired through the application of both knowledge and understanding that are refined and en-hanced with experience, over time, in an appropriate environment. As the appropriate environment did not exist in Engineering UK it was clear that such understanding and skills would not be developed by senior managers simply as a matter of course. This was a fundamental problem in the implementation of the scheme.

Although this was recognized, the day and a half spent on developing the essential understanding of mentoring was clearly inadequate, as there was too much for the mentors to understand and change in too short a period.

Responsibility and authority

It was encouraging that senior management recognized that the new strategy could only be delivered by the workforce and that by target-ing the development programme at supervisory level, they were hoping for the desired change of culture – 'bottom up'. However, this placed great responsibility on this level of employee who had no experience of the 'bottom up' concept and without senior management support and understanding would stand little chance of achieving it. This situation was an example of management handing over respon-sibility to the workforce but retaining authority over them – the typical problem of autocratic management. A leadership culture hands authority to people but retains responsibility.

Although a leadership culture was the desired outcome of both the development programme and the mentor scheme, it could not happen as the 'old' culture was too strong.

Interestingly, the model of the old culture was supported by the actions but not the words of the parent company. The language was that of development and change, but the behaviour, in the form of their dictates, was that of the past. Senior management behav-iour needed to change in line with the language, but, as it didn't, the mentors took their lead from the behaviour of their masters and simply carried on as before.

And speaking more of change

It is clear from the abundance of slogans that Engineering UK wanted employee 'ownership' of the strategy, for their language was that of empowerment and ownership. But, language is only the first step and if it is not supported by clear actions to demonstrate its meaning, change simply becomes a management fad in the minds of the workforce.

For example the term 'client' used to describe the learner or mentee has confusing and misleading meanings. This term implies a customer–provider relationship and seems to be born out of the 'customer led' concept. The term may be an attempt to alter the nature and conduct of existing relationships within Engineering UK and the mentoring dyad may contain some elements of this form, for example dedication to 'customer' needs, commitment and trust, but most writers would support a form of the 'trusted counsellor and guide' definition of mentoring put forward by Gladstone (1988).

There are a number of interpretations of the Engineering UK situation here. First, it may be that the mentors were incapable of changing their behaviours in line with this definition. Secondly, it may be that they did not understand the behavioural implications of the definition. Thirdly, this definition of mentoring may have been inappropriate in this situation, and finally, it may be that mentoring as defined above was not the relationship that they wanted to develop and therefore it was an inappropriate use of the term. This is fundamental, for if the terminology is incorrectly used or misunderstood, behavioural confusions will inevitably follow.

Further evidence of a mismatch between the language and the behaviour can be illustrated by a comment made by a supervisor who sums up the problem very succinctly, 'You can talk about development as much as you like but if the product is not out the door on Friday, you get your backside kicked.'

The informal use of language by management gives clues as to the real culture of Engineering UK, ie 'belly up, kick arse, break butt' and when talking about going to the factory floor, 'visiting the animals'. These expressions reflect underlying 'macho' attitude towards the workforce and reinforces management's position of control and command. They also illustrate that the actions as implied by the 'new' language are not matched by 'new' behaviour and a 'new' informal language has yet to emerge.

Development minded?

Lack of mentor skills was another factor. This was manifest by the confusion over counselling and coaching. Coaching somebody who requires counselling is simply the wrong approach. This confusion created conflicts and resentments in the minds of some clients.

Another factor that contributed to the demise of mentoring was the tendency of macho-management to undervalue people-development (their own included as macho managers believe they don't need development). This was evident through the mentors agreeing that mentoring was a good thing in principle but when it came to giving the time to their clients, they found it difficult to justify to themselves and seemed unable or unwilling to make the time available. Also, they would not give up time for further mentor training for themselves. They were being driven by short-term imperatives of production rather than the longer-term objectives implicit in the 'customer led' strategy typified by their slogan 'in it for the long haul'.

In a wider context than mentoring the attitude towards development can be further illustrated by the fact that the UK training manager needed to constantly persuade plant managers to release people for training. The end result of this was a compromised situation where people were released for training for shorter periods than necessary and the time span between training interventions increased. As a consequence this may have reduced the effectiveness of the training which in turn would fuel the negative attitudes towards training that already existed within Engineering UK.

Selecting mentors

Mentors were selected from an approved list and then paired with clients on the basis of controlled choice. This, again, is an example of the company heavily controlling a process which would be better managed by allowing some scope for personal choice.

Some mentors were paired with clients 300 miles away. This created serious communication difficulties.

De-skilling concerns

The issue of de-skilling continued as a concern. People who found their skills replaced by technology remained resentful. As some mentors did not give the time for discussions, these resentments were not resolved and the lack of trust in management continued. In the minds of the workforce, change equated with their either losing jobs or becoming de-skilled.

International dimension

The desire to achieve the common approach around the world and in different cultures is perhaps a misplaced ideal. People may find it difficult to alter their attitudes and behaviour for cultural reasons, and indeed, the desire of the parent company to push the strategy through simply served to support the 'macho' culture in the UK. As a result this culture was compounded and consolidated, rather than becoming altered as was intended.

All things to all people

The expectation of the mentor scheme in the UK business was too great, particularly in terms of the sheer number of responsibilities placed on it. It seemed as though the scheme was not only the driver behind substantial change, but also the mop for any other organizational people-problems that existed in Engineering UK. This contributed to the decline of what essentially should have been a well-planned and well-organized scheme.

The words of change were in place but the actions did not match them.

References

Clutterbuck, D (1992) *Everyone Needs a Mentor*, IPM, London, 2nd Edition.

Gladstone, M S (1988) *Mentoring: A Strategy for Learning in a Rapidly Changing Society*, Research Document CEGEP, John Abbott College, Quebec.

Kram, K E *Improving the Mentoring Process*. Training and Development Journal, April 1985, 40-42.

Video reference

BBC Training Videos (1994) *Managing Performance*, BBC Enterprises Ltd, London.

8. GETTING STARTED AT THE INSTITUTE OF MANAGEMENT

Neville Benbow, Head of External Policy and Chair of the IM's Mentor Review Group

This case study records the development of a mentoring process within an organization, from initial discussions through to the first six months of operation. It is too early to measure the success of individual mentoring relationships, but first indications are included in the study.

Why start mentoring in the first place?

We decided to embark on mentoring initially as part of our desire to achieve Investors in People accreditation. Mentoring was one of a number of procedures and practices which we decided to introduce as an integral part of 'IMPEL' – Institute of Management Providing Excellence through Learning – to show what we are doing to develop ourselves and the organization, hopefully going beyond the requirements of the IIP standard for the benefit of all.

It seems blasé to say that we did not need to carry out any research into mentoring or to employ an external consultant to help us on our way, but both individually and from an organizational context, we already knew a great deal about mentoring. As a professional management institute with a strong emphasis on individual and organizational training and development, a number of our key staff had extensive knowledge and experience of mentoring – ranging from personal experiences prior to joining the IM to helping other organizations to establish their own mentoring schemes on a consultancy basis.

Scope of the scheme

The scheme is open to all staff, irrespective of their grade and location. It is entirely voluntary – it simply wouldn't work otherwise. The scheme is intended to help individuals to realize their full potential – for their benefit as well as that of the organization.

Clearly, not everyone feels the need for the support of a mentor – many are happy to rely on their line manager or friends within the office environment. Mentoring is not, however, seen as a substitute for the relationship with an individual's line manager, but as a supplement to the activities of managers in developing their staff.

To date, ten members of staff have asked for mentoring and have been allocated the mentor of their choice. This equates to less than ten per cent of overall staff and is about on par with our initial expectations. When others realize the benefits that this group are deriving from the scheme, we can expect to see an increase in interest. Word of mouth will clearly be our best advertisement!

Marketing and review

Before the decision was taken to embrace mentoring throughout the organization, a draft paper outlining the scheme was circulated to all staff for comment on both the content and the underlying concept. The scheme aroused a considerable amount of enthusiasm from staff and managers at all levels and it was decided to roll it out, taking account of a number of suggestions for fine tuning the scheme.

The scheme could not get off the ground until all volunteer mentors had been adequately trained. A series of comprehensive training workshops – run by experienced IM staff – were held. Given the importance for top-down commitment, all the directors were trained in mentoring. So far, two members of staff have opted for a director as their mentor – the same director in both cases. It was decided that a Mentor Review Group (MRG) should be established to administer and monitor the scheme. Five volunteers were sought, all of whom were trained mentors, to serve on this group. Subsequently, two members of the group have left the IM: both have been replaced, one by an existing mentor, the second by the IM's careers counsellor, who is very experienced in mentoring but, because her role involves mentoring on an ongoing basis, is not a mentor within the scheme.

With the initial training completed and the MRG in place, the scheme was ready to be launched throughout the IM.

The MRG first met to satisfy itself with the efficacy of the mentors who had volunteered their services and had successfully undergone training. It was agreed that the MRG would meet mentors on a regular basis and that all new potential mentors would be formally interviewed by at least two members of the group, prior to training being undertaken.

Once all the procedures had been completed, as Chairman of the MRG, I wrote to all staff advising them that the mentoring scheme was now fully operational. A number of individuals had already expressed a desire to be mentored and I undertook to speak to them all individually to establish who they would like to be their mentor, subject to availability. In all cases, their first choice was both available and willing to act as their mentor.

Subsequent to the launch of the scheme, reminders of the scheme's availability have been made every two months via the IM's internal newsletter, and all managers have agreed to remind staff during personal development discussions of the benefits of mentoring.

Getting a mentor

Clearly it is important that in the same way that individuals have the right to select a particular mentor, mentors themselves have the right to decline to take on certain individuals for any reason. Capacity is always a potential problem – mentees are always advised that this may be a problem and they are asked to nominate a second choice in case their first choice cannot be accommodated, for any reason.

Staff wishing to be mentored are encouraged to approach the Chairman of the MRG in the first instance to start the wheels in motion. Once an individual has agreed to take on a mentee, it is then up to them to speak to the individual concerned and make any necessary arrangements. This initial point of contact is important; it enables individuals to have a reference point should things not go as planned and it ensures that you can advise individuals who want further details of the scheme or want advice on the choice of a mentor. It also ensures that the administration of the scheme is kept up-to-date. Details of mentoring arrangements are confidential between the mentor and the mentee – within the IM, the only obligation the mentee has is to advise their line manager that they have decided to have a mentor. The decision as to whether they divulge any other information is entirely up to them. The discussions between mentor and mentee should always remain strictly confidential.

As with any type of discussion or interaction, individuals only get out of mentoring what they are prepared to put in. Mentoring pairs can choose to agree learning objectives or they can remain totally flexible, working through issues as they arise. It is up to the mentee to decide how they wish to proceed. The process is for them, although it is envisaged that the mentor will find the relationship rewarding and that it will assist them in their own personal development.

If a mentoring arrangement is not working, either for the mentee or the mentor, either party should not be afraid of saying so. The MRG is available to help mentees and mentors alike, if required. Admitting that a mentoring relationship is not working is not a weakness – it's a strength!

The MRG is the backbone to the scheme, its support structure and review mechanism. At the outset, it was agreed that the MRG should meet not less frequently than every six months to review progress and, if necessary, make changes to the scheme. However, in the early stages, it was felt necessary to meet more frequently and to this end, meetings are held every two to three months. The group is currently discussing the possibility of introducing 'induction mentoring', which was suggested at one of our meetings. The aim of this would be to assist and support new members of staff, as an adjunct to the formal induction process that is undertaken by the individual's line manager.

Aims and objectives

All staff have received full details of the aims and objectives of the mentor support scheme. Clearly, it is important for the scheme to be designed to match the individual needs of the organization. The overall aim of the IM scheme is to improve the performance of IM staff, thus ensuring the achievement of the Institute's Mission and strategic plans. There are five key objectives:

- ☐ to improve and maintain the skills and morale of IM staff

- ☐ to provide a source of skilled guidance and support available to each individual member of staff

- ☐ to supplement the activities of managers in developing their staff

- ☐ to help staff to achieve the realization of their career development plans

- ☐ to improve internal communications.

Scheme progress and problems encountered

It has not been necessary for any amendments to be made to the organizational structure as a result of the decision to embrace mentoring. All managers and directors have committed themselves to the mentoring scheme, actively encouraging their direct reports to take advantage of the scheme. This is clearly crucial if the scheme is to be successful.

Fortunately, no specific problems have been encountered with the scheme, nor has it been necessary for any individuals to request a change of mentor. Current mentors have been invited to an informal discussion with members of the MRG before our next meeting, to obtain feedback and any suggestions for improvements to the scheme. We will also be asking mentees to complete a confidential questionnaire on the process, their experiences, the value of mentoring and any suggestions they have for improving the scheme. In the absence of negative feedback to date, we remain confident that the scheme is progressing well.

Fit with training and development plans of organization

Mentoring is complementary to the organization's training and development plan: for some individuals, it will be an integral part of their own career development plan. The identification of training needs is a crucial part of every manager's responsibilities. It is a two-way process: mentoring can be seen as a key training need for some individuals, whilst specific training needs can be highlighted by the mentoring process.

Limitations of mentoring

Clearly, mentoring will not always achieve everything that individuals want it to achieve. It is not designed to supplant the normal relationship between managers and those working for them. It is complementary to the management process and is designed to help individuals to realize their full potential.

The primary limitation of mentoring is where there is a lack of commitment from line management – not everyone wants a mentor, but those who do should be actively encouraged to have one. Line managers need to support their staff when they say they want a mentor – it is not an indication that they have failed as a manager, but it shows a commitment by the employee to develop themselves. Fortunately this is not a problem within the Institute. The mentoring relationship is often very different from that of line manager/subordinate and the decision should not only be supported but actively encouraged. If it works well, everyone is likely to benefit – the employee, the manager and the organization (and hopefully the mentor too!)

Discussion

Voluntary scheme. Mentoring can work in any organization with effort and commitment (at every level). It needs to be properly communicated and available to all. It must be voluntary and confidentiality must be assured.

Consultation. Organizations wishing to embark on a mentoring scheme will find that to gain commitment they need to discuss and consult with their staff and managers at every stage of the design and implementation. Managers may see mentoring as striking at the heart of their authority – if they are fully involved, they will see it as a benefit and wholly complementary to the line management process.

Steering group. Having the MRG is an important part of quality assurance and a delicate but firm process for assessing the suitability of mentors.

9. ASDA SUPERSTORES: MIDDLE AND JUNIOR MANAGEMENT MENTORING

Julie White

Asda Superstores is a £ multi-million retail organization, with over 200 stores nationwide. The organization, under the leadership of a recently appointed management team, has been undergoing a programme of restructuring and reorganization in the past year that is designed to re-equip the business for the increasingly difficult environment of the mid 1990s. The focus has moved away from short-term profit objectives, and many of the initiatives being undertaken are concerned with laying the foundations for recovery. In order to reduce the organizational weaknesses, which had until 1993 been evident inside Asda, a comprehensive programme of change has been adopted, to renew and alter not just the people and structures, but also habits and ingrained behaviour. A greater emphasis is being placed on the contribution and 'quality' of the employee, particularly at management level, in creating a more competitive business. There has been a reduction in the levels of management in the organization, management styles are becoming less authoritarian, measures are being taken to increase communication at all levels, and a common sense of values and direction is being developed among the management group based around the idea of a business focused on the customer and their shopping needs. The entire strategy is focused on changing the more traditional approach to retail taken by the Asda group in recent years, towards one of an organization better able to cope with the competitive nature of the business environment of the 1990s.

As a result of this strategy, there is an increasingly heavy emphasis being placed on the training and development of store managers, who are each in charge of outlets with annual turnovers of more than £200 million. A new management team brought with it new ideas and initiatives of how to correct the underinvestment in the organization and people. One of these was the idea of mentoring, which it was hoped would facilitate and enable the transferral of the company's new objectives, and help contribute to the development of the 'quality employee'. Top management were receptive to this idea as a potential way forward.

Store managers were given the extremely clear message from the company that they were expected to be two things: first, good leaders, and secondly, coaches for the people for whom they are responsible. The question was how could new store managers be trained and developed in the best and most efficient way. Mentoring provided the answer here. For who better to help the new store managers than those who already operated in the environment? When the situation was researched by the personnel team it was found that a basic system of informal mentoring had in fact already existed inside the organization at this level for many years, and what would be required was a formalization of this, with the Asda House and Regional Management team having the opportunity to target those who would receive mentors. In the past, the general store managers had selected individuals themselves, which had led to the underdevelopment of those trainees.

Once the decision had been made to adopt a mentoring programme, an external consultant worked with the personnel team to facilitate and oversee its implementation. Mentors were selected on the basis of criteria established by the training and development team: a potential mentor had to be 'a good manager, with a sound knowledge and understanding of Asda's way of working', and a 'good coach'. Although these criteria were somewhat vague it was thought that they would suffice. The mentors were told that the scheme was essentially experimental, and that they were therefore responsible for feedback and alterations to the programme. It was felt unnecessary to sell the idea of mentoring as most store managers were flattered at being asked for assistance and for their participation in the programme. Mentors were then given a one-day training session in order to communicate the general aims, and the regional personnel managers were given the task of monitoring the new relationships, with the training team providing back-up as required. There was no separate structure established for the management of this new development.

The first company review took place three months after the setting up of the pairs, and took the form of a meeting with the mentors and mentees to discuss the success of the relationships. Other items on the agenda were the aspects of the scheme that were working well, those that needed improvement, and the potential areas for development and expansion. At such an early stage the initial success of the relationships was judged purely upon the interpersonal success of the relationships. At this stage the majority were proving fruitful in the opinions of both mentors and mentees involved.

The benefits of the introduction of the scheme were seen to be manifold, although at this early stage the true extent to which the organization has and will benefit is difficult to ascertain. When trainees were leaving the programme and taking up their posts as managers it was felt there was a great advantage to be achieved from the support and advice function provided by the mentor, reducing the feeling of uncertainty and doubts sometimes experienced by new managers. The balance of one mentee per mentor was felt to be correct, as anything more would demand too much of a manager's time, and make unrealistic demands upon him or her. Additional benefits were seen to be that specific types of people could be targeted, trained and developed to be effective communicators of the company values, and people could potentially perform better and faster due to an increase in self-confidence.

Problems with the scheme largely stemmed from confusion that resulted around the lack of comprehensive briefing as to the purpose and objectives of the scheme, and its marketing to those involved. Some confusion was also evident as to the exact role of the mentor, particularly when compared with the training specialist. The mentees also felt that it would have been better if they had been briefed fully with their mentors. It was felt that the confusion had arisen largely as a result of the lack of preparation that had been undertaken by the Personnel and Training Team in the assimilation and communication of data to parties involved.

(In practice, the fact that other members of the organization were left in the dark as to what the mentoring scheme actually was, and involved, has generated interest and commitment in other areas within the business. So, although it is essential to inform participants of the exact nature of the programme, leaving some degree of mystery to surround the mentoring programme had worked to the advantage of the organization.)

As a result of these comments, Asda has now incorporated a number of changes into the programme, which new recruits will be party to. All managers, whether directly involved in the scheme or not, and the new recruits will be fully briefed on the objectives of the mentoring programme, together with their mentors. The pairs will be briefed on all aspects of the scheme under the eleven headings outlined below.

We can use these to effect a number of practical suggestions for those wishing to employ such a scheme in their organization. Before starting any programme of mentoring ensure that all the relevant parties are briefed fully as to a number of factors:

☐ what mentoring is

☐ who the mentors will be, and why they have been selected

☐ what purpose mentoring will serve in the organization

☐ what the potential benefits to all parties involved are

☐ how pairing of mentors and mentees will occur

☐ how the mentoring relationship will, or is likely to, evolve, including an outline of its structures and possible guidelines for behaviour

☐ the responsibilities of both the mentor and mentee should be clearly outlined

☐ the relationship between the mentoring pair and the training specialist

☐ the length of the relationship, including guidelines for termination (voluntary or otherwise)

☐ the potential problems involved

☐ how the mentor and the mentoring relationship will be appraised

☐ who else would benefit from mentoring.

The personnel and training team is now challenged with identifying pockets of people in other areas of the organization who would benefit from a mentoring relationship, and with setting up a scheme to meet their needs.

Discussion

Asda's scheme was set up in haste and therefore missed out on some of the important steps of preparation:

Educating mentees in what to expect and how to manage the relationship.

Selling the concept to those excluded from the relationship.

To some extent, an organization undergoing rapid cultural change will always find it difficult to keep everyone informed. However, Asda has clearly learned from its pilot programme.

10. SVENSKA NESTLÉ: MENTORING OLDER MANAGERS USING RETIRED BUSINESS PEOPLE

Jöran Hultman, project leader and consultant,
While the race is running project

Svenska Nestlé has a staff of approximately 2300 and is situated in the south of Sweden.

In the early 1980s a project was launched in order to safeguard the *young* talents within the company and to give them the possibility of development. This was also when the company started mentoring. Each one of the juniors was assigned to an older and more experienced person whom they could consult and use as a discussion partner.

This project was so successful that it now is permanent. It has had a significant impact in producing skilful leaders and specialists.

The question arose, 'What are we doing for the somewhat older employees?' We were obliged to answer, 'Not much really'. That is why the project *While the race is running* was started. It aims to let the company's employees of age 45 and over grow as human beings; to give this group a chance to stop for a minute, to think and to reflect upon their work and private lives. The project is designed to help those older employees to be motivated and committed to their work, to give them a new spirit and to widen their capacity.

Material for personal development based upon self analysis was specially made for this project. Lectures and discussions about stress, leadership, organizations and society, and other topics were prepared and delivered.

About 20 executives were chosen for the first group. In Stage I they had the opportunity to reflect on their situation in life regarding family, future and work.

Stage II for this first group was that each of them was allotted a mentor, a speaking partner, whom they did not know beforehand, and who was wise and experienced.

External mentors were chosen, all with a genuine knowledge based on experience, common sense, a natural authority and status. They were first-rate people of business, skilful in their professions and good leaders: people who had reached so far in their own professions that they were able to listen to others. For this, age and wisdom was needed and all the mentors were around 70 years of age.

They attended a half-day workshop covering the following topics:

☐ mentoring in general

☐ the objectives of mentoring

☐ the mentor's roles

☐ expectations

☐ important questions

☐ practical advice.

Stage III for the group was a 3-day seminar. A number of lecturers were invited, specialists from different branches.

This seminar was like a wave of knowledge and understanding of life. It addressed non-material values, society, human values, new operation forms, internationalization, stress and leadership. This was in order to enable the participants to build a clear picture of themselves in this changeable world.

By attending this project the participants got the chance to pause and reflect on matters that one normally tends to run away from and elbow out. Participants learnt that there exists an inexhaustible source of power, energy and joy; that life prolongs as long as one lives, and that it is never too late to make an effort to achieve the things one really wants; regeneration and change is a good thing, an opportunity rather than a threat.

The mentors' observations on the project

The following are some comments made by the mentors at the end of the project:

> One must have experienced a lot, met many situations, been curious and willing to broaden one's own knowledge. Furthermore one must be interested in one's fellow beings.

> Mentoring plays an important role when someone is considering the broader issues in life.

If everybody had an experienced and wise person to talk to, a lot of mistakes could be avoided.

A mentor must first and foremost be honest. It gives the learner the chance to reconsider decisions.

We, who are approaching 70 years of age, have our careers behind us and we do not have to keep our noses to the grindstone. We have the time to commit ourselves to the learners. We have also a vast experience to share with them. Furthermore we do not compete with anyone. We can stay impartial and be fairly objective without letting ourselves be influenced by accidental occurrences or different moods.

As a result of this project, individual development plans have been made for the learners regarding work, family and life in general.

The outcome of the seminar was excellent. The participants pointed out the following good effects:

☐   clear goals in work and family life

☐   obtained a qualitative expansion

☐   gained a better balance between work and leisure

☐   greater disposition for change

☐   improved leadership, eg a better listener

☐   gained the power and joy for renewal and development

☐   obtained an inward security.

The mentors have been immensely important to learners during this activity. They have been a great support, good listeners, open-minded, honest and confident with experience, maturity and self-knowledge. They have also been reassuring for the learners, helping them build their self-esteem.

The fact that the mentors were external was thought by most to be a good thing. This meant that there were no political considerations or preconceived opinions to worry about.

Following the success of this first group, which is very important for the company, a commitment has been made to establish a second group.

Results of the programme

Among results recorded by participants were:

- □ *qualitative expansion*: to dare as a human and as a leader and to get a better perspective as a whole

- □ *balance in work and leisure*: understanding the importance of balance

- □ *clear changes*: awareness of the importance of, and develop inclination to, clear changes

- □ *clear goals*: for work and for family life

- □ *present situation good*: reinforcement and security in knowing that one's situation at work and socially is good

- □ *a better leader*: and a better listener

- □ *strength to cope with one's own change*: to actively contribute to the change of one's working situation

- □ *inner strength*: to be able to make demand upon one's boss, and to have the power to move abroad with joy for regeneration and growth.

Participants most commonly felt that the relationships were:

- □ affirmative

- □ valuable

- □ developing

- □ thought-provoking

- □ a personal uplift.

Says the company:

> Not everyone has made dramatic changes and moved to a new job, but we have noticed a new spirit and an increasing effectiveness among all the managers who participated. The work runs more smoothly. We have appreciated the advantages and the profit in backing the mature members of the staff with time.

Discussion

Using retired mentors. This example of using the wisdom of years offers a challenge to many organizations, which currently seem over-ready to chuck people the age of the *learners*, in this case, on the scrap heap.

Cultural questions. In which other countries would retired mentors aged over 70 be respected? Does the 'yoof' culture in Britain for example, preclude the possibility of valuing people of this age?

Focus on life issues. This case places a strong emphasis on a holistic view of life: embracing purpose, home and work, joy, personal empowerment and a long-term perspective.

11. LANCASTER PRIORITY SERVICES TRUST: MENTORING FOR INDIVIDUAL, TEAM AND ORGANIZATIONAL DEVELOPMENT

Michael Green, Managing Partner, Transitional Space

This case study describes how one NHS Trust, in association with an external consultant, developed and implemented a unique mentoring project for the individual, and top team development of its executive management team. One of the objectives was to see how individual, and team mentoring could aid organizational development.

The NHS Trust has since been commended by a recent audit for its effective management and its proactive approach to change.

Background and context

Lancaster Priority Services NHS Trust provides three major services: general community health; mental health and services for people with learning disabilities in both hospital and community settings. Each division has joined the Trust at different times and whilst each was fully supportive of the Trust as a whole, each had their own way of working without too much sense of a 'corporate body'. At the time of the mentoring project it had been formed for less than a year.

The mentoring project was initiated some nine months into the Trust's existence. Once Trust status had been attained, a series of development workshops were run. These had proved valuable in bringing together the team for the first time, but were less successful in their prime objectives of individual development and the alignment of top managers.

David Jordison, the Chief Executive, and John Mercer, the General Manager (Manpower) felt that individual and team development of the executive management team (EMT) would result in a top management team better equipped to meet and master the challenges of change which lay ahead. Specifically this included the contraction and closure of one of the Trust's two hospitals; the contraction in one area and expansion in another of the mental health division; the increasing focus and expansion of the community services division; the threats posed and opportunities afforded by the dynamics of the market-place; and how the estate department that serviced both the Priority Trust and the Acute Trust could be fully integrated into the new culture.

The Trust's proposal was concurrently to develop the individual skills of members of the executive management team whilst promoting the development of the management team itself, at the same time ensuring individual and team needs were linked to the needs of the Trust as a whole.

Objectives of mentoring project

The objectives of the project were:

☐ to develop the individual skills of the members of the executive management team

☐ to develop the executive management team

☐ to develop individuals and the team towards the needs of the Trust.

It was intended that the end result would be a close knit management team with a substantial degree of mutual trust and a common interest in strengthening the effectiveness of the team as a whole.

The project was to be carried out initially over a period of four calendar months and project objectives met through:

☐ identifying organizational, team and individual needs

☐ generating developmental plans for the individual, team and organization, and strategies for implementation encompassing ways to overcome potential barriers

☐ implementing development plans in line with agreed timescales.

Approach used

The objectives were demanding and with good reason. The issues facing Lancaster Priority Services were challenging and the Trust required as effective an EMT as possible. Previous experience had taught it that a groupwork approach on its own would not be sufficient to address individual needs; likewise, an individual approach could not be guaranteed to address the team and organizational needs and issues. An integrated approach of both individual and group development within an overall organizational perspective was needed. Another factor was the peculiar position of NHS Trusts – public sector organizations, embodying one set of values, exposed to the marketplace, embodying a different set of values. There was an imperative to find an acceptable fit.

The project proposal that provided the best fit with the Trust's needs was one that used individual and team mentoring. It was felt that an external mentor and facilitator would be more appropriate in the circumstances. The level at which mentoring was required – at the top of the organization – meant that it was difficult to use someone from within the organization who had the credibility, the objectivity and the confidentiality required. The external consultant defined mentoring as the use of business and psychological interventions to coach, counsel and challenge, for individual, team and organizational development. The uniqueness of the mentoring relationship is that it creates a trusting environment in which the client works on his or her own development issues and explores the underlying hopes, anxieties and fears that constant change inevitably triggers, which, without the mentoring relationship, encroach into work performance and team relationships.

Typically, *individual* sessions might focus on:

☐   individual skill development

☐   coaching on live management issues

☐   the role of the individual in the group's development

☐   personal performance plan

☐   the individual's contribution to the team.

Team sessions need to have two agendas:

☐   identification of the major team and organizational issues that the team needs to address and the strategies to tackle them.

☐   focus on how the team is going to maximize its effectiveness in addressing the tasks.

This approach called for a considerable time commitment. Over the four-month period there were to be fortnightly individual sessions lasting between one and one-and-a-half hours and four group mentoring sessions which lasted between a half and a whole day each. The consultant used as a resource a team effectiveness profile and a management competency profile to aid the process.

Team effectiveness profile

The team effectiveness profile (TEP) (available in UK from Management Learning Resources Ltd 01267 281661) was developed to assist individuals and groups in identifying blockages to their group's performance. Richard Beckard suggested dividing possible group issues and blockages into five categories, which appear in the TEP (Figure 1). Individuals record their perceptions of their group's functioning, which are then aggregated for the group as a whole. The individuals can then compare their perceptions with the rest of the group and the group can compare itself alongside healthy and unhealthy organizations.

The TEP led the individuals and then the group to reflect on the results, differentiate between what is a particularly individual perception and what might be done to improve the group's functioning within these categories.

Management competency profile

The competency profile was a simple questionnaire, culled from a variety of sources and research, see eg Pedler *et al.* (1978), which categorized levels of management skill, eg personal management; middle management; executive management, and ranged from areas such as time management through the management of conflict to having a helicopter perspective.

Individuals were required to self- and peer-assess, and also get feedback both from boss and subordinates. The subsequent data was then used as a platform for deepening awareness and setting personal development plans for action.

Group mission: Healthy organizations and their sub-systems have compelling visions of the future and clearly defined and well-communicated statements of purpose.

Group roles: In highly effective groups, work is organized to support the group's function. Roles, relationships, and accountabilities are clear to everyone.

Group operating processes: Groups that have effective operating processes have consciously examined each policy and procedure by which the group functions for efficiency and effectiveness.

Group interpersonal relationships: For effective teamwork to occur, interpersonal relations must be of high quality. Each group member needs to be fully interactive with every other group member. A high level of trust is required if problems are to be solved and group work is to be satisfying.

Intergroup relations: One of the most serious drains on organizational energy results when departments or divisions of the same organization compete inappropriately. Win-lose situations need to be changed to win-win situations.

Figure 1 *Five categories of team effectiveness*:
(from Team Effectiveness Profile)

Mentoring model

The stages in individual, team and organizational growth and development are well documented, tried and tested, see eg Erikson (1977) and Schein (1970). The aim of the mentor is to make the transitions through these stages smoother and faster. Mentoring, in this project, is the focused application of psychological interventions to further organizational understanding, growth and development. It uses a combination of management development, psychotherapeutic and organizational consultancy skills.

Every step forward towards more competence, accomplishment and effectiveness is generally preceded and also followed by doubt, uncertainty and limiting beliefs about the self, engendered by past experiences, current reality and future concerns. The mentoring model focuses on these regressive trends outside the normal line-management function and thereby allows progression within the job to continue and accelerate. The inevitable reactions and resistances to change are thereby greatly reduced, allowing individual and corporate goals to be achieved more quickly and effectively.

Three basic principles in this model are to support, educate and challenge, be it the individual or the team, in the endeavour to grow and develop.

Integration

The opportunities afforded by both individual and team sessions were to allow individual and team development to occur in the respective sessions and at the same time for individuals to have the opportunity to discuss interpersonal issues outside the group, in a safe and confidential environment, to gain clarity over the particular issue and decide on the most appropriate ways to resolve it. This could then be raised at the next group session if deemed right. The trust built within one forum would transfer to the other.

The process and the outcomes

Group sessions

Mentoring is traditionally seen as a one-to-one process. Within the context of this project the group of people who were being individually mentored were also working together as the executive management team. The team sessions were run as typical team-development workshops with the added value of individuals having reflected upon and planned what it was they wanted from the workshops within their individual sessions. Subsequently the individual mentoring sessions were used to debrief and reflect upon what went well, what the individual could do differently and how they were going to action the next steps.

The team-effectiveness profile scored the executive management team as being on the borderline between a cohesive group and an effective group, just edging into the latter (Figure 2). Group roles were seen to be most effective, followed by group mission and group-operating processes. Group interpersonal relationships were highlighted as being somewhat ineffective, and further down still were intergroup relations.

Immature group: A collection of individuals who have not begun to develop the group task and process skills. They are dependent on the appointed leader for direction and support.

Fragmented group: Conflicted by a number of issues that it needs to resolve before the group members can work together effectively.

Cohesive group: Developed strong interpersonal relationships and allegiances. Independent thinking is not particularly valued; the danger of groupthink is high.

Effective group: Developed both task and process skills. In general, the group members work well together, although there is clearly room for improvement.

Synergistic team: Highly developed and interdependent. The group members coalesce as a true team or function brilliantly as super-stars. Often their team decisions go well beyond what the individuals working by themselves could hope to achieve.

Figure 2 *Overall team effectiveness*:
(from Team Effectiveness Profile)

Four group sessions were held (three half-days and one full day). The sessions had the purpose of teambuilding through focusing on interpersonal relations and expectations of each other; the effectiveness of the team as a whole; how an effective management team will ensure success in developing the organization in line with its strategic direction; and generating a detailed action plan of managing the necessary change within Lancaster Priority Services to achieve its vision.

Major issues which arose during the first three sessions included:

☐ the need to review and reflect upon the previous year's performance (both task and process) and to improve in all areas

☐ how the enthusiasm of the team to achieve the vision *right now* created considerable pressure on itself and on individuals, which needed to be managed

☐ how the EMT had a compelling vision across the Trust but needed to communicate this more fully

☐ the need for greater support between team members

☐ the need to align other groups (eg the Trust board and the divisional management teams) with the EMT, the business plan and the strategic direction.

The group sessions themselves increased the willingness of the team members to support each other. All the above issues were tackled and action plans to deal with them put into place. Organizationally, the EMT identified the critical nature of ensuring that the necessary changes over the next three years were well planned and effectively implemented across the Trust. This was the focus of the final session where the team looked at what systematic, structural, functional, strategic and interpersonal changes needed to achieve the vision, and the way this would be effected.

Experience is what managers have and do. It includes observations, decision-making processes, activities, behaviours. It is the grist for the mill, so to speak, of the mentoring session.

The *review* of experiences within the context of the 'bigger picture' and who one is (identity) is a vital part of the learning culture. It is only by pausing for reflection on what has gone well and what can be improved can individuals and teams move forward. Reviews were carried out on an individual and team level.

The next step was to *develop* ideas, strategies, behaviours and creative solutions into a more efficient and effective way of doing things.

Integration is the key to success of any development initiative and confirms that true learning and development has taken place. Individuals and teams need to integrate their new perspective, be it skills, knowledge or attitude, into new behaviour within the organization. Integration needs to be carried out with a knowledge and understanding of the 'big picture'.

The *big picture* in this context was how external forces impinged on the individual, team and the Trust's development and how the individual, the team and the Trust could influence the big picture.

It is the context in which any changes will be made and the realization that the client organization is by necessity an open system, which itself is within a larger system. For the individual the bigger picture was generally the executive management team, and the vision and mission of the Trust, all within the context of the changing environment of the NHS.

Benefits and learning

The project met all of its stated objectives and the benefits that accrued are outlined in Figure 3.

The General Manager (Manpower) believes that there are many lessons to be learned from this kind of project, not just for Trusts but the NHS as a whole and other organizations generally (Figure 4). He says:

> A successful project for top team development depends on a number of variables. The team obviously needs to be ready to undergo change and there has to be an organisational need for development. We obviously had that need – the tremendous challenge of managing change. I believe the attitude of the team and the Chief Executive to commit to change however painful or fulfilling it may be is a crucial point. It was interesting to note here that some of the EMT members were won over to the concept of individual and team mentoring as the project progressed, and they were as much surprised at themselves as the rest of us were. It was the combination of individual and team interventions which added a whole new dimension to the development process.

The EMT's readiness to trust in the process and allow for the time it can take for the process to work, played a crucial role in getting results. The process worked because it had that balance between structure, direction and clear objectives on the one hand, and flexibility, commitment to getting at the truth and sheer persistence by the team on the other.

Having established a clear direction and a way to achieve the vision the executive management team have continued to use individual and team mentoring as part of their process of reviewing and developing themselves and the Trust.

Project benefits were collated from individual and group evaluations.

Individual benefits
1. each participant became more aware of themselves, their colleagues and the dynamics of the EMT
2. each participant reported greater clarity of vision and direction, in relation to themselves, the EMT and the Trust
3. time out for thinking through the issues produced more strategically minded decisions
4. behaviour has changed in a number of respects to cover the broad spectrum of management style and healthier (ie more support and more challenge) interaction with boss, peers and other staff.

Team benefits
1. the team process has improved; individual members are feeling more confident now that the EMT is working as a team, aware of the group process and committed to the whole process
2. the EMT has clarity of vision and a clear direction for itself and the Trust
3. the EMT has increased its efficiency and its effectiveness in all aspects of its purpose.

Trust benefits
1. increased clarity of vision and direction
2. greater alignment between the Trust's constituent parts and movement towards corporacy
3. greater ability to manage change.

Figure 3 *Project benefits*

There needs to be a readiness of the team to undergo change, be it a sense of dissatisfaction or a sense of untapped potential.

There should be an organizational need for development, in this case the tremendous challenge of managing change.

The attitude of the team and the Chief Executive to commit to change however painful or fulfilling it may be.

The understanding and skill of the external consultant to move the team on, as individuals and as a group.

The combination of individual and team interventions adds a whole new dimension to the development process.

When dealing with barriers to performance, and the subsequent discussion of personally confidential issues, the use of an external consultant is vital.

Clear and challenging objectives provide a real focus.

Whatever individual and team issues emerge, always see how they link to the development of the organization.

Be prepared to trust in the process and allow for the time it can take for the process to work.

Don't overplan; ensure flexibility of structure to allow for emerging themes.

Figure 4 *Learnings from the project*

Discussion

Is team mentoring possible? The process described here is clearly broader than coaching in that it covers a wide spectrum of activities and issues other than job tasks. It allows for confidential discussions and perhaps even the development of close friendships. However, there is a significant potential (if not actual) conflict of interest between the development needs of the individual and those of the team. Is openness about fears, ambitions and insights possible in these circumstances?

Mentor learning. The relationship described seems to hold few opportunities for learning by the mentor – a critical part of the richness of a 'full-blown' mentoring relationship.

Mentoring top managers. This case emphasises that people at the top of organizations need to be mentored by an external mentor.

Definition of mentoring. The fact that developmental relationships of this kind are becoming increasingly common indicates that there is a need for them. Whether they are strictly mentoring or not is less important than whether they deliver real developmental benefits.

References

Erikson E (1977) *Childhood and Society*, Paladin, London.

Pedler M, Burgoyne J and Boydell T (1978) *A Manager's Guide to Self Development*, McGraw-Hill, Maidenhead.

Schein E (1970) *Career Dynamics: Matching Individual and Organizational Needs*, Addison-Wesley, Reading, MA.

12. BREAKING THE GLASS CEILING AT
AER RIANTA, DUBLIN

David Clutterbuck

Aer Rianta manages three international airports at Dublin, Cork and Shannon, in the Republic of Ireland. The company places a high value on people and this is reflected in the company's core values of excellence, customer service, humanization, and open management systems. Since 1981 Aer Rianta has been at the forefront in addressing the issue of equal opportunities. In 1982 an affirmative action co-ordinator was appointed to implement a programme of equal opportunities for both men and women in the company. The company has taken many initiatives over the years to further its equal opportunities objective. These include the introduction of job sharing in 1981; flexible work hours system, paternity leave and career breaks in 1982; workplace child care facilities in 1984; spare time study, equal opportunities and personal development training, among others. Specific programmes aimed at management, people with disabilities, secretaries and personal assistants, encouraging women into non-traditional areas such as trades and airport police and fire service.

Its initiation into mentoring came about as a result of a 'Women in Management' project set up in 1992. At this time an analysis of women's representation throughout the organization revealed that there had been an influx of women into management in the previous two years. While this change seemed momentous (as it often does when it is long in the offing), it had taken over a decade for women to gain only 14 per cent of the total management positions in the company and most of these were at the lower management levels. It became clear that while considerable numbers of women were entering the company and progressing to junior and middle-management positions, senior management remained an exclusively male preserve. Aer Rianta recognized the importance of this group of women to the furthering of the company's equal opportunities objective to have a gender-balanced management profile. While this would inevitably change with time, Aer Rianta wanted to ensure that the process occurred as quickly as possible. For this reason it was decided to focus on the experiences and needs of this particular group of women to ensure their future development and the development of the women managers to follow.

The company's chief executive, Derek Keogh, and Sheila Flannery, the manager of equal opportunities development, based in Dublin, brought a group of these women together to discuss their experiences and identify barriers to progress. Issues that arose included access to information, opportunities to participate in more senior management tasks, access to training and development and exposure to decision-making. They then facilitated a further meeting, this time with the senior management team, to explore what could be done to overcome the barriers.

Derek Keogh, all senior managers and women managers participated in a process of identifying existing and potential barriers to women's progression and participation at management levels. One of the solutions to emerge was an 'understudy' programme, where women managers would be paired with more senior male colleagues to learn by observation and discussion. As these proposals were developed, however, it was quickly recognized that much more was required, and the scheme was renamed 'mentoring' to reflect this. Following the seminar and workshops the combined group devised an action programme that included identification of individual training needs of women managers, formal training programmes, networking and mentoring.

Aer Rianta's mentoring programme was launched in January 1993 and involved 18 women managers being mentored by senior managers in the company. Participation by all of the senior managers (mentors) and women managers (mentees) was on a voluntary basis. The objective of the programme was to provide an opportunity for women managers to gain from this developmental process of mentoring, a process which seems to develop almost naturally and informally for many men. The launch programme involved a half-day training programme for mentors. Then mentors and mentees met over lunch and arranged their first formal appointment. Mentees received a half-day of training on mentoring also. The launch was facilitated by an external consultant. Individual training needs analysis carried out for the women provided a basis for identifying their personal objectives for the mentoring programme.

Sheila Flannery and a senior colleague attempted to match mentors and mentees as closely as possible to the mentees' individual needs. Factors taken into account included whether the mentee would benefit most from someone from an unrelated area; and the practicality of matching someone from one airport with someone on another site. Sheila Flannery asked mentees who they would prefer to be mentored by and tried to make use of those declared preferences. However, some mentors were not suitable – for example, those who were mentees' direct line managers.

All mentors and mentees were volunteers, having been asked by letter if they wished to participate. Of the senior management team, all but one volunteered, the exception being a manager whose job involved so much overseas travel that he could not be sufficiently available. Three-quarters of the 24 eligible women managers signed up.

Mentor and mentee were given a diary to record their experiences, but most made little or no use of them, preferring to find their own ways of managing the relationship. However, says Sheila Flannery, 'A couple of mentors did say that every time they saw the diary on their desk it served as a reminder of their responsibility.'

The women's progress was monitored at Dublin Airport through network lunches of the Women in Management group, and telephone contact with mentors. At Shannon Airport mentors and mentees gave feedback through other channels, the main conduit for this being the local equal opportunities officer. Progress was also reviewed through feedback sought at the three modules of a Women in Management training programme.

Some relationships blossomed quickly; others never got off the ground; yet others faded away as circumstances changed. One mentor was concerned that the relationship seemed to be going nowhere; that the mentee appeared to have lost interest. On investigation, Sheila found, through patient questioning, that the real problem was the size of the hierarchy gap – the mentee was simply too reluctant to take up the mentor's time. Once the issue was in the open, the mentor and mentee were able to discuss and resolve it, putting the relationship back onto a firm footing.

By mid-1993, it was time to review where the scheme had got to and what could be done to boost it. A full-day review session was planned with the European Mentoring Centre and, as useful input to that event, mentors and mentees were asked to complete a questionnaire about their experiences. The survey found that both mentors and mentees agreed about the importance of listening as a core mentor skill, although mentors tended to rate giving encouragement higher than mentees did. It also found that career progression was the least significant benefit. (This may well have been simply because too little time had passed for many of the women to have achieved promotion.) More important were achieving greater realism, gaining exposure to other levels of the organization, increasing self-confidence, general maturing and faster learning of political skills.

Mentors generally felt it easier to establish a relationship of trust than did mentees, with none of the mentees saying they found it very easy. The most frequent topics of discussion were planning learning opportunities and career issues.

In the review session, the women managers opened up more specifically about the nature of the relationships with their mentors. Revealing comments included:

> One of the main advantages is learning about another area of the company through my mentor.

> The challenging aspects of the relationship are very important but you will only see these if the relationship is equal.

> I've become more confident and can hold my own more. I have a better knowledge of the company. Observing my mentor, I notice that he doesn't have all the answers but has the technique and confidence to carry on.

> My mentor was generous with the quality of our meetings but not with his time.

> Time management was a disaster in the beginning, but it has improved.

The discussions emphasized the importance for the mentees to be motivated to work out and push for what they wanted from the relationship – in other words, to take an active role in managing the relationship. Although the issue of being mentored by someone younger than themselves was raised, most of the women did not see this as a problem for themselves.

Mentors' comments included the following:

> We had no agenda and no objectives. We managed the relationship by discussing each other's work and different management styles.

> One of the benefits of mentoring is how it forces you to stop and think about your own managing techniques.

> It was difficult building the relationship with my mentee and after about 10 meetings, I felt we had both run out of steam. There was nothing to talk about any more.

Mentors and mentees agreed together that the scheme was worth continuing, and that increased effort would be needed in each relationship to set clear objectives to work towards. Critical components of a successful relationship were seen to be:

commitment	trust and confidentiality
openness	clear objectives
encouragement	developing a career path
investing time (not just in meetings but in preparation and follow up)	feedback sharing experience questioning
demonstrated interest	the mentor being a critical friend

Above all, the review emphasized the need to give the mentoring process time to develop and establish itself.

One of the primary benefits is confidence, which many of the women gained. 'It was largely because they had been recognized as having potential and that the company had placed importance on their development,' Sheila explains. 'The amount of time given by senior managers was evidence of this'.

> Another benefit was that mentoring helped overcome communications barriers. It gave them access and insight into other layers in the organisation. It showed them that they could do these jobs, that there was no mystique about management. Some of the women have come back to me after applying for more senior jobs, saying that without mentoring and other training initiatives, they would never have had the confidence to go through the selection process.

Since the scheme began, four of the mentees have been promoted and many of the others are seen to have increased their potential sufficiently to be candidates for promotion in the next few years. One now works directly for her former mentor and the relationship continues, though adapted to the new circumstances. A measure of the success is that male managers at the same level as the women mentees have now asked to be included, and this is about to take place.

The mentoring scheme was an experiment, and one which the company has learned from. Among the key lessons, Sheila says, are:

Firstly, the chemistry between two people is something you can't anticipate, even though you may match the mentee's weakness with a mentor who is strong in that characteristic. The two people must be compatible types, able to build rapport and get on together. We could possibly have intervened a lot earlier in relationships where that wasn't happening.

It seems to take longer to build rapport in cross-gender mentoring. However, having a cross-gender mentoring scheme on an official basis has made it legitimate within the organisation for men and women to help each other in developmental relationships, so it should become easier in the future.

Secondly, we now realise how important it is to have the time to support individuals and to monitor regularly how they are getting on. This was difficult, but without spending time providing support through tips and guidance some wouldn't have gained so much benefit from the relationships. It takes a lot of time to keep in touch with people on an individual basis and this needs to be planned into the programme at the start.

Discussion

Cross-gender issues. Mentoring can get off to a relatively slow start if the parties involved are not fully clear about what they are trying to achieve. Cross-gender issues can become more of a barrier in these circumstances, especially where there are no women available to act as mentors. Mentoring programmes for women need to recognize that there may be greater reluctance by the mentees to trespass on the mentors' time. Mentors need to be sensitized to the difference in perspective and expectation of the female mentees.

It will be interesting to observe over time the extent to which these issues become less significant as mentoring becomes a more accepted part of Aer Rianta's culture. Are these special difficulties simply a reflection of the current organizational culture or a more general distinction between the sexes?

13. OXFORD REGIONAL HEALTH AUTHORITY: MENTORING NEW BOARD MEMBERS

David Clutterbuck

The creation of National Health Trusts as part of the Government's reforms of the National Health Service (NHS) meant that many people, who had no previous experience of being a director, suddenly found themselves serving on boards of trustees. The structure of these boards is statutory and consists of five executive directors, five non-executives and a non-executive chairperson.

Many of the newly appointed executives had relatively little top management experience, having been, for example, clinicians or senior nurses. By the time the third wave of trustees was being prepared, in 1993, the Oxford Regional Authority decided to help these executives acclimatize to their new jobs by providing additional intensive management development though a Top Management Programme. Central to this programme was that each of the 100 participants should have a personal development plan (PDP).

Time to develop PDPs would be short – less than three months – so the participants needed help. Rather than provide a central resource, Gary Hoyte opted instead for a mentoring scheme, in which the mentor's role would be to act as a sounding board, helping executives think through their objectives and how they would achieve them. The mentors could also:

☐ be role models

☐ challenge the executives' assumptions about themselves and their careers, and

☐ continue to help the executives as they worked on implementing their PDPs.

The executives were asked to find their own mentors and were given some written guidance on how to do so. Some found suitable mentors within the NHS region; some in the NHS but outside the region; and some outside the NHS entirely. The mentors were invited to attend an intensive half-day training session, which covered the nature of their role and how to manage the relationship.

Results

The project was evaluated by questionnaire six months later. Replies were received from 30 mentees and 18 mentors. Among the most interesting results:

☐ most mentees (70 per cent) found it easy to obtain a mentor; no-one found it difficult. Almost all had a clear idea of what they were looking for in a mentor. The most common characteristic sought was 'experience in executive management in the NHS' (77 per cent), followed by 'coaching and counselling ability' (70 per cent), 'good network of contacts' (57 per cent) and 'a good political operator' (50 per cent)

  In seeking advice on how to identify and approach a suitable mentor, they used working colleagues and/or the region's own HR consultants

☐ three out of four mentors were flattered at being asked

☐ most mentors and mentees felt it easy or relatively easy to establish a relationship of trust

☐ mentees generally thought that responsibility for managing the relationship was shared at the start – mentors generally thought they took on the initial burden. But both agreed that the mentee usually took on the management after a while

☐ both mentors and mentees saw the most important roles of the mentor to be:

  – sounding board
  – listener
  – critical friend

  Mentors also scored 'giver of encouragement' very highly

☐ time pressures were the most serious problem for mentor and mentee

☐ the number of times the mentor and mentee met over the nine weeks varied from just once to five. The most common was three

☐ the most common mentee benefits, as perceived by the mentees themselves, were: 'faster learning of political skills' and 'greater realism'. Mentors also pointed to 'greater self-confidence' and 'enhanced ability to cope with new situations'

☐ the most common benefits for mentors, in their opinion, were 'satisfaction at seeing someone else grow' and 'learning they acquired in the process'. Mentees added extension of the mentors' networks as a perceived additional benefit

☐ all the executives had developed PDPs

☐ asked 'Would you do it again?' 100 per cent of responding mentors and 90 per cent of mentees said 'yes'.

Discussion

Time period. Mentoring can work over a very short period, if there is a very focused goal to work towards. A significant factor in this case is the relative maturity of all the mentees.

Finding their own mentor. Senior people, established in a discipline and of an age where they already have a store of their own experience to draw upon, had little difficulty in either finding a mentor or making good use of the relationship.

Mutuality of benefit. The strong consensus about the benefits for each party from the relationship suggests a fairly high degree of rapport.

14. ICL LEARNING CONSULTANCY: A LOOK INTO THE FUTURE

David Megginson

Systems integrator, ICL, has long been at the forefront of human resource development, and a recently introduced use of mentoring by the company's learning consultancy may point the way for many more organizations in the future.

The ICL Learning Consultancy offers learning solutions within the ICL group. Its mission is to enable ICL to achieve its crucial capability shifts.

It has in recent years moved towards a project-based organization structure where the old notion of a 'boss' has been disappearing. Individual ICL learning consultants have increasingly been selling their services to project leaders, who are now called managing consultants. At any one time individual learning consultants may be working for a handful of different managing consultants. The relationship is not one of subordinate to boss however; it is much more that of a supplier of professional service to a client. There is a resource manager who assists individual learning consultants/administrative staff and in commissioning managing consultants to allocate the staff resource, but the resource manager is emphatically not seen as the line manager of the consultant. Don Wilde, a learning consultant, says 'I provide my portfolio of Assessment Centre activities to the managing consultants for young entrants, for high potentials and for project management; and self-managed learning facilitation to the managing consultant for management.' He feels personally in control of this process, and the resource manager's role is to support any clearing of excess or shortfall in supply of consultancy service, as well as providing the information and control infrastructure.

ICL Learning has followed the logic of this development through to the point that 1995 will be the last year in which appraisal will be carried out in a conventional way by each consultant's notional boss. Even in 1995 the customary planning, monitoring and reviewing of what development the consultant will pursue following the appraisal will be carried out not by the boss, but by the individual consultant supported by a mentor of their choice.

In 1996, the process will be taken further. The boss will wither away altogether, and individual consultants will get their data for appraisal from 360° feedback from senior staff, clients, customers, colleagues and junior staff. Further input will come from objective reviews conducted with the managing consultants owning each objective. The learning consultant will then discuss the input with their mentor, whose primary role will be to help the consultant to understand and rationalize the feedback, and produce their own appraisal form as a result of this discussion.

Even pay determination – the last bastion of the power of the line manager – is being taken away. In 1995, the salary review for all staff was carried out via a single meeting of the two senior partners, the resource manager and the personnel manager. Pay rises were determined, based on performance and perceived market value, with inputs provided by previous bosses. In 1996, there will be no boss input; pay rises will be based on the strength of each individual's contribution (to the business of the managing consultants) and on the views of their colleagues, although the actual mechanics of this process have not yet been defined. This process acknowledges that peers often know more about performance than anyone else, and will be an interesting example of extending the logic by enabling the best-informed people to have a significant say in the consequences of this information.

The line manager is dead; long live the mentor? Too early to say, perhaps, but the signs are interesting.

There are a number of other points about the mentoring scheme that model best practice. A particularly striking feature of this scheme is that not only will all permanent staff have a mentor, but associates, temporary contract staff and catering staff are also invited to have one.

Mentors have to come from ICL Learning Consultancy if they are to fulfil the responsibilities we have outlined, but there is nothing to stop an individual having a second mentor from outside the division, in addition to that required by the scheme.

Staff are asked to choose and approach their preferred mentor, who may be a peer, or be superior in experience or role, but is unlikely to be less experienced. Those approached as mentors should feel able to decline if they feel that the relationship will not work, or if they have accepted as many requests as they feel they can resource.

The initial meeting is seen as crucial and is to be used to set the tone and parameters for the future. A case is made for formally agreeing and recording the ground rules or contract. This could include points about confidentiality, scope of the relationship, allowable time demands and frequency of meetings.

Apart from the mandatory requirements for appraisal and the production of a learning plan, how the mentor is used by the learner is very much down to the individuals. This may include career counselling, problem resolution, personal issues or whatever. A principle advocated is that the initiative for these other elements should come from the learners and their needs, not from the mentor imposing a 'service'.

Confidentiality is seen as a key feature of the scheme and the mentor should not reveal anything learned in the mentoring relationship during the pay determination process, for example, unless in the presence of the learner and/or with the learner's permission. The mentor's role is not to sit in judgment on the learner, but to encourage learners to propose ideas and make their own decisions.

Mentors are offered learning workshops to develop their skill in carrying out the role, and they are encouraged to seek support in carrying it out from colleague mentors or indeed from their own mentor. The possibility of a mentor support group or network for ideas is being examined.

ICL are monitoring the scheme, including the use of an opinion survey of both learners and mentors. It is intended to add real value to the development of individuals and be seen as 100 per cent opportunity and zero per cent threat.

Discussion

Mentoring centre stage? Is this case a sign for the future, that mentoring may be on the point of moving from being an attractive add-on to becoming a core part of the web of relationships at work?

Following natural relationships. This scheme is a clear example of where the formal process follows the pattern of successful informal relationships, with the learner taking the lead, and a great deal of choice being afforded to both parties at every stage.

Mentoring for all. ICL's approach is also interesting in that not only are all the permanent staff involved, but also associates, people on short-term contracts and contractors are also offered an opportunity to participate.

Mentor support by networking. Although formal training is provided for mentors, they are also offered a framework of support through networking and peer relationships. This accords with our experience that mentors learn well and value a chance to talk about their relationship and their part in it in confidence and with people who are in the same boat.

PART 3
Individual Cases

3
INDIVIDUAL CASES

INTRODUCTION

One of the revelations for the authors in recent years has been the diversity of people who have the capacity to be effective mentors. We have seen autocratic managers turn out to be remarkably empathic and helpful to people who are prepared to challenge what they say and do; poorly educated people become superb mentors to the educationally or socially disadvantaged; and people of low personal confidence who have blossomed as they reap the benefits of helping someone else. The busiest managers have found time to spend helping more junior colleagues to reflect – and have enhanced their own learning from doing so.

Mentors and mentees have made successful relationships across cultural divides; geographical distances; age and gender differences; even extremes of personality differences.

Why some relationships 'click' and others do not is still largely a mystery. Every time we think we begin to understand it, new insights and experiences demonstrate that we do not.

What we do know is that:

☐ working together on a common problem enhances growing together – the more the mentor can show an interest in the mentee's specific learning opportunities (without taking over) the more rapidly rapport grows

☐ mutual respect is a critical ingredient

☐ strong initial rapport does not necessarily lead to the greatest learning. In the diagrams below, box A is likely to lead to the most rapid rapport. But these two people have least to learn from each other. Most learning will come in box D, but these two people may never be able to communicate effectively.

Similarity

A	B
C	D

Personality, learning style

Dissimilarity

Similarity	Dissimilarity

Background, discipline and interests

The most beneficial mentoring relationships, therefore, often take place in boxes B and C. It usually takes a mature and insightful mentor/learner to manage a relationship in box D.

☐ age and gender are only a barrier where one or both people feel uncomfortable

☐ the mentor need not be more senior than the learner (in UK-style mentoring at least). The case of Lesley Martinson illustrates this clearly. What counts is the *potential for transfer of relevant experience*.

Those readers who have experienced mentoring first hand will recognize themselves in some (or perhaps all) of these cases. For the authors, gathering the cases has perhaps been most beneficial in demonstrating what more we can achieve with our existing mentoring relationships.

1. AN EXECUTIVE MENTORS A BLACK UNDERGRADUATE: SHIRLEY JOAN COLLIE WITH MOHAMED TAKOLIA

Norman McLean, Director, National Mentoring Consortium

Shirley Joan Collie, a British Airways business executive, and Mohamed Takolia, a then third-year BA Honours Accounting and Finance student at the University of East London, were matched through the mentor scheme matching process in autumn 1993.

Shirley Joan has a teaching background, and is experienced in dealing with young people in a learning environment. She has a knowledge of the problems that create a barrier to learning, and has good coaching skills. For Mohamed, it was her confidence, manner and high standard of professionalism that made her a successful mentor. Shirley Joan is a graduate with an understanding of the system, who knows what it is like to be on a graduate training scheme.

Setting objectives

Objectives were set through a two-way discussion at the first meeting based on Mohamed's perception of his own needs and informed by Shirley Joan's perception of those needs:

1. organization/time management for study
2. exposure to the world of work in a blue-chip company
3. teamwork and working on practical projects, learning about the business community and appropriate business language, social skills, dress, and so on
4. targeting particular career areas: what would Mohamed want to do and how would he get there.

Building trust

The relationship had openness and honesty from the start. Both Shirley Joan and Mohamed felt that they were lucky to meet someone with whom there was a natural rapport. It helped that it was easy for the mentee to identify with the mentor because of their closeness in age and backgrounds. Shirley Joan felt that it was particularly important to keep promises and deadlines that linked into the development of Mohamed's time-management skills.

Shirley's role was to set up meetings and to drive the relationship. She set meetings and time-planned, but on reflection would have given more of this responsibility to Mohamed. Mohamed felt that Shirley Joan was available to discuss any problems he might have, and Shirley Joan was keen to make her time available to him, and gave him her home phone number.

Both parties felt that Mohamed's reactions were very positive. He was very well respected by British Airways staff and gave a very good impression of himself and the mentor scheme. Shirley Joan said that it was a very positive experience for both of them.

What helped and hindered

Shirley Joan felt that her most positive behaviour was the self-analysis that she undertook in order to understand the learner's needs and to create empathy. For Mohamed, her positive points were her communication and time management, which he described as 'special'. He was also impressed by her discipline and orchestration of the relationship.

Shirley Joan considered that at first she was expecting too much of the learner. This was corrected and on reflection a more flexible approach was adopted. However, Mohamed felt that Shirley Joan was consistently helpful to him.

At first Shirley Joan was frustrated by Mohamed's lack of time-management skills, but generally there were no problems in the relationship on either side, and the pair related well.

Ending and beyond

In a sense the relationship has not ended, even though the official scheme finished in May 1994. Shirley Joan would have liked more follow up, but this was difficult because of Mohamed's exams and his move to his home town. She still considers herself to be his mentor, and is happy to discuss any difficulties or successes with him. For Mohamed the experience was a good one, which he did not wish to end. While there has been a gap in the pair's contact, Mohamed intends to keep Shirley Joan up to date as his career progresses.

Consequences

Shirley Joan thinks that the scheme took more time than she had initially imagined. It promoted her ability to self-analyse and examine her own life. She found that she was viewing herself from a different angle and giving herself good advice. She derived great satisfaction from successfully meeting a challenge.

Acting as a mentor occurred at a good point in her career – as a young graduate on a management training scheme it provided her with a chance to learn about people and the management of people.

Shirley Joan is now involved in a British Airways corporate mentor scheme with Thames Valley University, as a direct result of her work with the mentor scheme.

Mohamed's work with Shirley has increased his confidence in how to approach the business world, and has increased his appetite for success, which he feels he is now much better equipped to deal with. Mohamed says of the scheme, 'It's a good confidence-builder and a good way of understanding the world of business.'

Discussion

Fellow feeling. In this example, the fact that the mentor is close to the learner in terms of experience of being a recent graduate and of also being Black, is seen as an advantage.

Modelling. What mentors do in the relationship is every bit as important as what they say.

2. THE DIRECTOR AND THE GRADUATE TRAINEE: PHILL BROWN WITH CATHERINE MOORE*

'After wearing Doc Martens and jeans for four years, it came as something of a shock to have to put on a suit and a smart pair of shoes.' This response from Catherine Moore follows that of most graduates entering a new career in industry and being confronted with the realities of business life.

In her case, she was joining Yorkshire Electricity in September 1992 as a management trainee after graduating in biology and psychology and then spending a year travelling the world. Suddenly, the experiences of diving off the Great Barrier Reef or trekking in Thailand seemed to count for very little when compared with correct telephone manner or carefully selected shoes instead of DMs.

Yorkshire Electricity introduced a mentor scheme in 1992 to aid the sometimes difficult transition from student to manager and Catherine was allocated to Phill Brown, the 45 year-old boss of the company's new telecommunications division. He was perceived as a guide and counsellor for the new recruit.

Catherine and Phill were left to work out much of their mentoring relationship for themselves. 'We do provide some guidelines,' says Stephen Guy, personnel director, 'but essentially we want to avoid dictating too much. Otherwise, the relationship could become very formal and be regarded as just another part of the company's hierarchy and operations.'

First stages

Initially, the couple decided to meet every three weeks or so although, in the beginning, neither was very sure about what to discuss. 'At first, I talked too much,' confesses Phill, 'and I was too anxious to suggest that I *could* remember what it was like being a graduate trainee!'

---

*   This report first appeared in *The Mentor,* 2(6), October 1993.

This probably made matters worse for Catherine. All the management trainees had attended a full, first-week's mentoring induction course that she recalled as exciting and, at times, nerve-racking, because the importance of making a good first impression was stressed.

'Now, I found myself entering an unequal relationship', she remembers, 'meeting someone I had to work closely with, who possessed the advantages of experience, knowledge and seniority. In fact, the induction was quite intimidating and I thought it would be very hard to make a good first impression.'

Gradually the relationship developed and their regular one- to two-hour meetings became a forum for discussing the graduate training programme, company policies, office politics and people. Importantly, through these an understanding of in-house jokes and jargon became Catherine's informal barometer of assimilation.

She followed a broadly-based training programme that involved placements in different departments and it was this very variety of experience which emphasised to her the value of the mentor scheme.

'The placements give you experience and build up your knowledge of the company', she says, 'but each time you start in a new department, you're back to that feeling of ignorance and of being no great use to anyone. Phill thus became the constancy factor in my work and our discussions helped me see things in perspective.'

Differences

One difference from university life became apparent very early to Catherine. As a student, she worked for herself and her work had little effect on anyone but herself, but at Yorkshire Electricity, she discovered that she had to rely on others and that her work had an impact on what others did.

This point was illustrated in what Phill and Catherine both recall as the 'public enemy incident'. On departmental placement, she had repeatedly unpleasant experiences with a hard-pressed district supervisor from whom she needed information for a project. Her requests for help often provoked brusque and negative responses, which she found very frustrating.

'When out in a district office, being introduced as a management trainee from Head Office does not create instant popularity,' Catherine recalls.

Phill remembers that she was clearly disturbed by such responses. 'I thought it best not only to discuss the problems of difficult working relationships but also to suggest that these incidents were not necessarily typical or long-lasting problems. Hence my flippancy in remarking that because she disturbed other people's routines, she had become public enemy number one at district levels.' The comment worked and proved to be a perfect icebreaker, based on experience, which reduced the incident to its proper perspective.

Benefits

So, was all the benefit of the mentor scheme one way? 'Obviously, there was an imbalance,' says Phill, 'it wouldn't be a mentor scheme otherwise. But it is still true that often the most innocent questions are the most difficult and Catherine certainly made me think hard on occasions.'

'Having to accommodate our meetings into a busy diary was also good for me and proved to be very refreshing. The idea was supposed to be my giving Catherine some overall perspective, but in practice, I was doing that for myself as well.'

Although officially the mentor scheme lasted for only a year, Catherine hopes that contact will continue on an informal basis; if it does, both would consider that to be a distinct mark of success.

Discussion

Informal mentor development. In this case natural processes were left to set the level and nature of the relationship. Although there were some difficulties, it seems to have worked well in this case.

Mutuality of benefit. Although there is a large disparity in experience, both parties express having gained from the relationship.

Life transition. Preparing people for the world of work is one of the major life transitions, and mentoring is exceptionally valuable in these circumstances.

3. PEER MENTORING, SUPPORTED BY A CONSULTANT: JANE SMITH WITH JOHN JONES

Bob Garvey

This case study presents a tool that may help human resource practitioners and mentors to understand the dimensions of mentoring relationships more fully. This research tool can be used to provide the basis for initial mentor/learner discussions and it can also be used to help resolve difficulties that may arise during the relationship. Mentoring is a dynamic process and therefore individual pairs change over time as both develop within the relationship. This case study tracks some developments over time. The study also mentions the use of learning styles, see Honey and Mumford (1986), in a mentoring situation.

Explaining the dimensions

As a consequence of the uniqueness of mentoring relationships, each specific pair may feature different combinations of the dimensions. Theoretically, it may be possible that certain combinations of the dimensions are present in a mentoring relationship that are absent from other types of relationship. It is also possible that some of these dimensions must be present for the relationship to be an effective one.

The dimensions are opposite points of a continuum as follows:

Open ———————————— Closed
Public ———————————— Private
Formal ———————————— Informal
Active ———————————— Passive
Stable ———————————— Unstable

What dimensions mean

Open. If the relationship is an open one the two parties feel able to discuss any topic in a free atmosphere. There are no 'off-limits' subjects.

Closed. In a closed relationship there are specific items for discussion and an understanding that certain issues are not for debate.

Public. In a public mentoring dyad other people know that the relationship exists and some of the topics discussed in meetings may also be discussed with third parties.

Private. A private relationship is one of which other people are not aware, or at least only a limited or restricted number of people may know about its existence.

Formal. A formal mentoring relationship is one that involves agreed appointments, venues and time scales. It is one that may be part of an 'officially' recognized scheme within an organization. This does not mean that the content and behaviour of the parties in the relationship are formal but rather, the relationship's existence and management are formalized. The members of the partnership in this formalized relationship are likely to establish ground rules of conduct.

Informal. The informal dimension is one where the relationship is managed on a casual basis. There are unlikely to be ground rules. The parties are likely to work in close proximity to each other, as this tends to encourage a 'pop in anytime' foundation for the relationship. The informal dimension relationship can operate in both a wider social context and within an official scheme. Informality does not describe the content or behaviours in the partnership, but its structure and organization.

Active. An active partnership is one where both parties take some sort of action as a result of the mentoring discussions. This may take many forms from, in the case of a mentor, an intervention on the learner's behalf, or in the case of the learner, a change in behaviour or activity. Active can also mean that contact is regular.

Passive. A passive mentoring relationship is one where there is little action taken by either party as a result of mentoring discussions. Contacts between the parties may also have lapsed.

Stable. A stable partnership is one in which the behaviour of both parties has an element of security and predictability. There is an understood consistency and regularity that provides a feeling of stability. This may also be linked to a feeling of commitment. The element of trust is of great importance in this dimension.

Unstable. An unstable relationship is unpredictable and insecure. This dimension is a manifestation of some of the negative aspects of mentoring where trust and commitment may be lacking.

Time plays a crucial dynamic role in the mentoring process for as time progresses, the relationship may alter and different dimensions may emerge or come to the fore as a result.

CASE STUDY

The names of the people have been changed to protect their privacy and confidentiality.

Both parties in this study work for the Health Service. The learner is taking a part-time MBA course. The mentor's function is to support the learner during the two years of the course.

The Mentor

Name:	Jane Smith
Gender:	Female
Age:	32
Position:	Training and Development Manager
Learning Style:	Changing – developing activist leanings from a theorist base
Background	7 years' Health Service experience and 3 years' experience in Training in a commercial organization.

The Learner

Name:	John Jones
Gender:	Male
Age:	32
Position:	Surgical Services Management
Learning style:	Theorist
Background:	10+ years' Health Service experience

This mentor relationship has a number of interesting features about it. Namely:

1. The mentor is female and the learner is male. This makes it an example of cross-gender mentoring.
2. They are the same age.
3. They have a similar status in the Health Service. (Points 2 and 3 make this an example of peer mentoring.)
4. Initially they worked in the same Trust. They were then separated by about three miles because John was seconded out. John was then appointed to a new full-time post and the relationship has now ended as a result of chief executive action.
5. The relationship had acute problems but these were resolved.
6. Their respective learning styles had a significant influence on the relationship.

The mentor's view

After ten months of the relationship, Jane admits to finding the mentor relationship with her learner 'difficult'. She believes that John initially chose her for the following reasons:

1. They have quite a good working relationship.
2. John wanted somebody inside the organization.
3. John did not have a good relationship with the General Manager. (The GM didn't want him to do the MBA.)
4. Jane was a 'last resort' and he felt that she would not be so critical of him as others might be.

Reasons for agreement

Jane agreed to adopt the role in order to:

1. Develop her own understanding of mentoring so that she could implement a similar programme for other managers within the Trust.
2. Help John develop his understanding of work-related issues through the MBA

3. Provide John with career support so that he might be in a better position to gain employment outside the Health Service if he needs to. (Jane saw job security for John as a major issue.)
4. Help John to understand the difficulties he has with relationships at work so that he may develop into a 'better' manager.

The learner's view

John agreed with most of Jane's observations on the rationale behind his choice. However, he added the aspects of accessibility and availability, and the fact that he believed that Jane had a different knowledge and skills base to his own. At the beginning he felt that Jane had a 'head start in her understanding of the mentoring process'. The work relationships issue observed and identified (No. 4 above) by Jane was not discussed in the research interview with John.

Analysis of the dimensions

Open	Y		X	Closed
Public	Y		X	Private
Formal	X Y			Informal
Active	Y		X	Passive
Stable	X Y			Unstable

Mentor's View = X
Learner's View = Y

Figure 1 *Relationship dimensions*

Analysis using the tool places this relationship as a 'closed/open', 'private/public', 'formal', 'active/passive', 'stable' partnership.

The closed/open dimension

In their early meetings they agreed ground rules of conduct. John was keen to have a strong MBA focus but he did agree that other work-related issues could be discussed. Jane was particularly keen on this as she did not see her role as 'an extension of an MBA tutor' but rather 'as having an all-round development focus'.

At ten months into the relationship John's agenda, in Jane's view, had the upper hand and discussions around other developmental issues had not been forthcoming. She described the relationship as 'the opposite of openness', and John's agenda of their discussions as very controlled. At this time Jane was feeling a strong sense of frustration with John. Jane said, 'He loves to show me his assignment plans and timetables,' but she believed that he needed to widen his thinking beyond the MBA course, for his own good.

John's perspective was interestingly different. He believed that Jane's counsel on the MBA was exactly what he needed. Indeed, he believed that the relationship was progressing along the lines of the agreed ground rules.

Clearly, at ten months into the scheme the relationship had a problem. Jane was very frustrated in that she recognized aspects of John's behaviour as unhelpful to his career prospects and felt that she would be able to help him modify his approach through the mentor discussions. Indeed, at this point she was in such a state of despair about the deadlock that she was ready to withdraw from the mentor role.

This 'closed/open' split was a contributor to the deadlock in the relationship for, while John unknowingly controlled the focus of the agenda so tightly on MBA specific issues, the relationship, from Jane's perspective, had difficulty in developing. This 'closed' agenda was compounded by John's enforced move to another Trust. The potential for 'common ground' and 'common understanding' was reduced by the move as they no longer shared the same work place. This move and obvious threat to John's security may help to explain Jane's perception of John's determination to keep the agenda 'closed' although he felt that the agenda was 'open' and on agreed lines.

The private/public dimension

Jane may have put her own position at some risk by agreeing to adopt the role of mentor to John. This was because, despite the opportunity within the mentor scheme to include the role as part of her performance review, Jane did not discuss the role with her Line Manager (General Manager) or with the HRD Director. She believed that their response would be that, with John, she was 'wasting her time'.

This pressure to keep the relationship 'private' was causing difficulties for Jane in that she was not gaining any recognition or support for her efforts. Indeed, she might, if discovered, have received reprimand for starting and continuing the relationship.

Therefore, their meetings tended to be arranged out of office hours and in a neutral venue away from Jane's workplace. However, she was committed to the concept of mentoring and it was this commitment to both the process and John that kept her going. She appeared to have a 'started so I'll finish' view of the situation! John was unaware of this 'private' dimension and believed the relationship was 'public'.

The formal dimension

As previously mentioned, they established ground rules early in their mentor meetings. They agreed in advance meeting times, dates and venues. This dimension does not create any significant issues in the case.

The active/passive dimension

At the time of the initial interviews, John was clearly gaining as an active partner. He was, through Jane's obvious skill as a mentor, widening his understanding of MBA-related topics. John said that Jane 'helps me to step away from things and look at them in order to clarify a few things in my own mind'. He also confirms Jane's perception that the agenda was heavily controlled when he said that the relationship 'is pretty much logistical and about planning things'.

It was this that put Jane into a 'passive' role where she felt unable to influence or contribute to what she saw as priority issues for John. Namely, his response to change and his behaviour towards others. This 'passive' position for Jane was a key element in the deadlocked relationship and a contributor to Jane's feelings of frustration. This may be linked to the cross-gender issue.

According to Sheehy (1974) women do not follow the same type of life cycle as men. In general and traditional terms the first half of women's lives is linked to 'serving others'. This is manifest in 'serving children and husbands' (Gladstone 1988). In Sheehy's (1974) studies she observed that women with careers tended to opt for 'service'-based work such as teaching and nursing. Sheehy (1974) observed that the second phase of women's lives, when children are not so significant, tended to be one where dormant talents and greater creativity emerged.

Levinson refers to this influence as generativity and he sees it as the strong factor in women's lives. This is reflected in the careers women choose as well as in their raising families.

Sheehy (1974) believes that the key difference in the behaviour of men and women is best described by the words 'initiating' for men and 'responsive' for women.

This debate is generalist in nature in that neither one behaviour nor the other is exclusive to men or women, but our culture, though changing, still develops initiation in men and responsiveness in women. This responsiveness may go some way to explain Jane's role as 'passive' and John's initiating behaviour may explain his role as 'active'. Jane listened and responded to John and did not initiate further debate despite appreciating the need. John believed that the relationship was balanced. However, Jane felt that the 'passive' role was unsatisfactory for her and did not fulfil her needs in the relationship. The relationship was unbalanced from her view point.

The stable dimension

During the ten month period of the mentoring partnership with Jane, John was seconded to another district and subsequently seconded again to another Trust in yet another district. These changes were part of a restructuring programme within the 'home' Trust. John would not get his original job back because it no longer existed.

The secondments had a time limit on them and so, in reality, John was facing redundancy if he didn't find another position. John admitted that Jane was a strong stable influence in his life through these disruptions. He also admits that he felt 'very bitter and upset' by the changes and that 'Jane's ability to be objective about that and not take sides but to push me to think positively about it, was significant', and that she 'reassured me of my own self-worth'.

This type of outcome from mentoring is well documented (Gladstone 1988, Clutterbuck 1992). Stability is obviously crucial to John and Jane clearly enabled him to feel some security in uncertain times. As John puts it, 'I think that it has been useful at times in particular doing the MBA programme as being a sort of stability, and in a way Jane's done the journey with me ... It's been a bit of a constant which has been necessary.' It may be that this strong desire for some stability in a very uncertain situation influenced John into keeping the agenda 'closed' and focused. It could have been that the prospect of introducing his behavioural problems into the mentoring discussion may have threatened his security further. He may have controlled the agenda in order to preserve his security.

Jane now recognizes this but at the time it didn't change her feelings of frustration in the relationship. She was able to recognize the role she was playing but she wanted to become more 'active' in areas other than those John would allow.

Evolution over time

At the start, some of the dimensions of the relationship could be plotted on opposite ends of the continuum. This may have contributed to a confusion of roles and purpose, in the mind of Jane in particular.

Time has influenced the dimensions of this relationship and through time the dimensions have evolved to create a new and quite different model.

This evolution was partly due to the willing efforts of Jane to make a success of her role and partly due to an intervention.

The learning styles intervention

Background

Jane believed that John's learning style was a contributor to his 'entrenched' viewpoint and a contributor to the creation of the 'closed' agenda in their relationship. She also believed that John's strong theorist style contributed to his behavioural problems with others. These manifested themselves particularly through John's reluctance to 'shift' his ground or be flexible about certain issues.

Jane said that John 'is a strongly principled person who sticks to his principles, no matter how small the issue'. It was this, she believed, that led others to believe that he is rigid and immovable.

It is interesting to note that Jane's learning style has its roots in the theorist style but, by her own admission, is changing through environmental necessities. She believes that she has been able to develop another style of learning and behaving that is more appropriate for a 'fast changing and responsive' Health Service. Jane is of the opinion that it is important in this environment to become more activist/pragmatist in style, particularly in her role in Training and Development.

Jane is clear that John is a 'nice person, very hard working and a good employee for any organisation' but he has become victim to a cultural change where 'outcome' has become more important than 'process'. This 'outcome' philosophy is one which is driven by targets and measurable end results. John's thinking was, as she understood it, locked into the ideology of the 'old' Health Service where the way things were done, regardless of the outcome, was important. She clearly understood John's position at the time of this first interview as it was one she could recognize in herself.

This may explain both her feelings of despair with him and her willingness to pursue the relationship. She felt he needed to be less resistant to change and more willing to adapt to the new climate for his own survival. As previously mentioned, John's previous bosses have little faith in his ability to manage in the changing climate.

The intervention

I suggested that at their next meeting Jane might like to re-visit the learning styles profile with John. During this discussion, Jane could use the focus of the profiles as a vehicle to introduce her thought that their relationship was deadlocked.

The profiles would provide the information and evidence that John needs, as a theorist learner, to understand the deadlock. Jane's view was that this was a make or break meeting and much would depend on John's response.

The outcome

Jane tried this approach at their next meeting with dramatic effect. She said that it 'opened up the discussion' and helped John to appreciate and understand the differences in their separate perceptions of the relationship. The learning styles profiles provided a neutral and factual reference point for both, which had the effect of keeping the discussion focused.

The meeting lasted for over two hours and both agreed that it was 'very productive' in that it helped to 'clear the air'. This enabled them to redefine their partnership.

Following this meeting they have had three further meetings at informal venues and Jane says that while the meetings retain an academic element, they are now able to discuss other issues concerning John's future. She also reports that over a period of six months, John seems more 'confident, outgoing, assertive and business minded'.

These observable changes in John have contributed to him gaining a promotion to a new job that he applied for in open competition.

At the time of the 'turning point' meeting, Jane discussed her mentor role with her own boss and gained his agreement to its continuation. This had the effect of changing the relationship from a 'private' dimension to a 'public' one. This must have relieved Jane of some pressure.

A final change in the dimensions of the relationship is that, as the discussions became more 'open', Jane moved from a 'passive' listener to a more 'active' partner in the relationship.

The final development

Following John's appointment to a new position, they continued the relationship until a chance remark brought it to an abrupt end.

Jane mentioned to her General Manager in passing that she was still mentoring John, to the response, 'you are not still wasting your time there are you?' He was adamant that since John was no longer part of the same Trust in any form, Jane should no longer provide the mentor support.

Jane's view was one of shock. The relationship did not have very much longer to run and John was about to enter a new phase of the MBA programme, the dissertation, and would therefore need continued support. She also felt that, 'after all, we are all still Health Service'. This was not the view of her General Manager, who instructed her to finish the relationship.

Stunned, she phoned John to tell him. He was 'very disappointed' and had, initially 'a great feeling of loss'. However, he understood the reasons and was satisfied with the relationship, and grateful to Jane for her support and guidance. He says that he 'learned a great deal from Jane' and that when he graduates he will include Jane as a major contributor to his success.

Jane, on reflection, felt she should have continued in her own time. She feels a sense of loss. She found the role interesting and challenging, which she now misses.

This situation could be an example of the negative elements of the Health Service 'marketization'; Trusts view each other as competitors. This means that collaboration is not welcomed and represents a clear break with the former traditions.

John agrees with this view in principle although, in his case, he sees the problem more of the fact that the General Manager was 'glad to be rid of him'.

Conclusion

It should be acknowledged that the changes in John over time can be attributed to a number of factors: the threat of redundancy and consequent feeling of insecurity; his desire to adapt to the Health Service changes to survive; a series of limited secondments and the influence of the MBA course. However, the one work-related constant through this period was his mentor. Jane's influence must have contributed much to his development. She provided him with support, guidance, coaching (specifically in interview techniques for his new job) counselling and honest feed-back. Jane was also a 'neutral figure to bounce ideas off'. It may be significant that this neutral position was the one truly independent element in John's life. He said that he discusses work-related issues with his wife but sometimes there is 'too much emotion involved with the possible insecurity that the conversation generates'.

This case example demonstrates that a mentor relationship can transform itself provided there is the will on both sides. Jane needed to change her approach just as much as John did. Gladstone (1988) suggests that 'successful mentors accept change willingly' and that 'mentorees are encouraged to devote their talents and energies to attainable goals and as a result they develop self-confidence.'

This seems to have been the case in this example. Jane's positive view on change and ability to assess her situation and change as a consequence enabled her to convey this view to John, with dramatic effect.

It also demonstrates the depth of impact that mentoring can have on the individual participants. The relationship evolved and changed to an 'open', 'public', 'formal', 'active' and 'stable' partnership.

Open	YX		Closed
Public	YX		Private
Formal	YX		Informal
Active	YX		Passive
Stable	YX		Unstable

Mentor's view = X
Learner's view = Y

Figure 2 *End result*

It may be that these are dimensions needed for an effective mentoring relationship. However, it is also clear that a combination of these dimensions and the elements of trust and commitment were crucial for the success of this partnership.

References

Clutterbuck, D (1992) *Everyone Needs a Mentor*, IPM, London, 2nd Edition.

Gladstone, M S (1988) *Mentoring: A Strategy for Learning in a Rapidly Changing Society*, Research Document CEGEP, John Abbott College, Quebec.

Honey, P and Mumford, A (1986) *The Manual of Learning Styles*, Peter Honey, Maidenhead, 2nd Edition.

Levinson, D (1979) *The Seasons of a Man's Life*, Alfred Knopf, New York.

Sheehy, G (1974) *Passages: Predictable Crises of Adult Life*, Dutton, New York.

4. MENTORING A PERSON WITH DISABILITIES: PATRICIA WITH PAUL

Patricia is a civil servant

Paul and I met several years before our mentoring relationship commenced. I was facilitating a disability consultative group which Paul attended as a participant. Our initial encounter was not a harmonious one.

☐ My perception of Paul was that he was a highly intelligent young man who had the ability to identify key areas to inform a debate but who was unable to express himself in that environment other than in a confrontative manner.

☐ Paul viewed me as the departmental 'mouthpiece' on equality and was less than convinced of my sincerity or commitment.

Both views were somewhat extreme!

A year after our first meeting we both transferred to the same relocating unit. I was a Senior Executive Officer in the unit and Paul was an Administrative Officer. Paul did not form part of my line management command.

Over a period of months we developed an understanding and respect for each other's values. We shared a common commitment, which was to further the interests of people with disabilities in the work place.

Mentoring relationship

Our mentoring relationship began when Paul started a positive action course called 'Unlocking Potential', for people with disabilities.

The package, which contains a number of self-development exercises, also asks participants to recall past experiences including episodes of discrimination and feelings of powerlessness, before moving on to develop strategies to deal with those situations in the future. The sensitivity of the issues raised means that although there is a need for line management encouragement, it is imperative that independent support is also provided. The mentor helps participants to work through feelings and emotions that come to the fore as a result of reliving past experiences.

Our contact

We agreed to meet at regular intervals while Paul was working through the programme. Our meetings started with Paul describing the activities he had undertaken from 'Unlocking Potential' and progressed into the more personal areas, for example the feelings engendered by the tasks and the coping strategies he felt he needed to develop.

Our contract contained a fair degree of flexibility. In particular, we agreed that if a meeting could not be arranged at short notice, Paul could contact me by telephone if there were important issues he wished to discuss.

Our intention was for the mentoring relationship to continue for the duration of the course and beyond that if we agreed that this would be beneficial to both of us.

Our aims

Our aims in establishing the relationship were:

☐   for the mentor to provide 'counselling' and support as necessary throughout the programme

☐   for the mentor to provide insights into the 'politics' of the department to enable the mentee to make more informed decisions

☐   for the mentor to provide a safe environment for the mentee to discuss work-related issues and form solutions to problems

☐   for the mentor and mentee to develop skills from the relationship that could lead to improvements in current performance as well as enhancing competences for future roles.

Difficulties encountered

The fact that I knew all the individuals in Paul's line-management chain presented me with my only difficulty. It was hard to put knowledge gleaned from personal observation of Paul's managers' behaviour to one side and offer objective advice.

However, Paul and I had discussed the respective roles of mentor and manager at the outset. We were both aware that it was not within my remit to influence management decisions on his behalf. My role was to help Paul:

☐ to work through key issues he had identified

☐ to develop skills to constructively confront difficult situations.

Lessons extracted

As a mentor, the following were key issues for me:

☐ never underestimate the value of the relationship between mentor and mentee

☐ never underestimate the time needed for meetings. Build in time to unwind, relax and discuss safe areas before moving on to the more difficult issues

☐ the need for effective dialogue between mentor, mentee, manager (and, where appropriate, trainer) before the formal relationship commences; this ensures there is no subsequent misunderstanding about respective roles

☐ the need for mentors to have a range of skills to equip them for their role (eg listening, questioning, 'counselling' and constructive confrontation skills).

Current relationship

Our relationship has developed into one of trust and concern for each other's well-being. From the start of our mentoring relationship, I was aware of the responsibility that I had undertaken when I had agreed, at Paul's request, to become his mentor. Although our meetings were structured, we shared some funny moments reflecting on past experiences as well as addressing the serious issues. This sharing of both humorous and serious episodes has helped our relationship to develop to its present status.

Although we no longer both work for the same organization we have maintained an 'informal' mentoring relationship. We contact each other regularly to discuss key issues in our careers. However, although we discuss matters relating to Paul's development, there is now a greater emphasis on mutual support and keeping each other apprised of equality developments – our pet subject.

Outcomes

Paul has become more clearly focused and deals with difficult issues thoughtfully and objectively. In return, I have gained some personal insights into the barriers that people with disabilities face in the workplace, as well as developing effective interpersonal skills. These areas feature prominently in my current post.

Discussion

Line manager link. This case illustrates the value of staying with the experience of the learner, rather than using information gathered from the learner's managers.

Mutuality. It is also a case where mutuality of benefit has developed over time.

5. MENTORING BY A YOUNGER, JUNIOR COLLEAGUE

Lesley Martinson, Cabinet Office

I asked a colleague to become my mentor when I began a 2-year advanced diploma programme for trainers that encouraged participants to seek mentors.

At the time, we worked in the same open plan office; she was several years younger than me and in a grade one below mine. Nevertheless, she had more training experience and was one of the few people to offer me direct and detailed feedback whenever we trained together. It was this quality that I valued most and sought to build upon during the mentoring relationship.

At the beginning of the programme we met to discuss our expectations. I do not remember her having many expectations of her own; she was concerned more with helping me to work out what I needed from her. I realized that I wanted her help in sharpening my learning performance and personal effectiveness. For example, I completed the Honey and Mumford learning styles questionnaire and then she completed one based on what she knew of me. By working through answers where we differed, I was able to gain insight into how my self-perception matched up with another person's perceptions of me. This gave me a more realistic starting point from which to develop.

She continued to give me feedback on the specific development areas I had targeted, either in the course room where we worked together, or in the office environment where I was working on my personal effectiveness.

She was particularly skilful at giving feedback. It was always detailed enough for me to get my teeth into and act upon yet she was not judgemental and supported me in taking risks in order to develop, risks which I may not have taken if left to my own devices. This undoubtedly speeded my progress.

Our meetings were irregular, but since we worked in the same office contact was frequent. Some meetings naturally followed on from a course on which we had worked together and were reviewing or, if I had been working with someone else, she would often be there after the course to listen to my self-assessment of what progress I had made. Formal, pre-scheduled meetings tended to be very irregular and probably only numbered four or five over the 2-year period, with less towards the end as I became more independent.

Meetings tended to be both intense and tiring yet, at the same time, full of laughter. Without humour I feel we could have become too precious about the whole process. One of the key benefits to me during the meetings was having her listen to me. She tended to say little, probing only when necessary. The process seemed to help me sort my thoughts and gain new understanding. I was surprised how powerful a medium mentoring proved to be in this respect.

About nine months into the programme there was an occurrence at one of the residential modules that left me feeling angry and powerless. It was my mentor I telephoned, and she helped me by allowing me to vent my anger and talk through my options. The support she offered was invaluable at this time.

A few months after the programme began I was promoted and moved into a new research and development job in the same branch. Several months later the branch was restructured and I became a training manager – this time with staff management responsibilities. My mentor was suddenly a member of my team of 12 people with a middle manager between us!

This gave rise to an immediate problem. I had to develop a new team, take forward a new work-load and continue my diploma. I didn't want to lose my mentor but realized that her line manager, and colleagues at various levels in the team, could well resent our relationship.

I decided to speak to her line manager and each team member individually. I described the work I had been doing with my mentor and explained that we had contracted not to discuss her manager or other members of the team. We had also agreed that she would not be privy to any organizational information that could not be made available to the whole team. I explained that if any one of them was in the least bit uncomfortable about the relationship, it would be dissolved. I would not attempt to allay their fears by reasoning them into submission!

I was concerned that people would not object to the relationship because they would not want to rock the boat, so I spent quite a lot of time stressing that it was OK to feel uncomfortable and there would be no comeback for saying so. In the event, they all seemed surprised I was bothering to seek their permission; some thought

I was making an issue out of nothing. The mentoring relationship continued until the end of the programme with no problems for the team.

My mentor accompanied me to the diploma award ceremony and eventually we both moved on to other jobs. I have just begun to mentor someone. It seems only right to repay the debt I owe to my mentor in this way. She will not see a direct benefit, but her investment will yield fruit elsewhere.

Discussion

Informal and formal. This is a splendid example of the blending of formal and informal. Lesley was invited to find a mentor as part of an educational programme, but she sought out the person that she wanted and established the relationship type.

Status. This case demonstrates that mentoring does not depend on status, that the mentor can in fact be less senior in hierarchy level. What counts is the learning that takes place.

Mentoring and line responsibility. It also illustrates the issues that can arise when mentor and mentee move into direct line responsibility; and how these can be handled through openness and sensitivity.

6. LONG-TERM PEER MENTORING: MIKE ALLEN WITH RAY HINCHCLIFFE AND OTHERS

Mike Allen interviewed by David Megginson

I came into the Employment Department as a Clerical Assistant, accidentally, from being unemployed, after an abortive attempt to become a teacher. So I have moved up from the bottom rung, and I know what it is like to be managed both well and badly. My peers now (Grade 5 in the Civil Service structure) tend to be very bright people, who have joined at a high level, so I emphasize people management, as this is the key thing inside me that differentiates me from them.

Throughout my career I have found it important to be able to go and talk to people: to ask 'How do I do this? How do you do it?' I have had variable success. One boss, three layers above me, was always prepared to explain why he was doing things. This was very valuable. If I had bosses who weren't willing to give the time, I had to reach out for others. In my career, I could usually find someone. Knowing the value of this to me, I have tried to do the same with others.

The longest mentoring relationship I have had is with Ray Hinchcliffe, with whom I have worked closely on and off since 1983. We are currently on the same grade, and so it is peer mentoring, and both of us benefit from it. We first met when I came to Sheffield on completion of a full-time MSc at Shrivenham. I was given a big project to deliver a new financial management system for the Manpower Services Commission. My team of four included Ray. I was completely lost; I knew about management and about the field part of the organization; but I knew nothing about accounting and little about large mainframe computer systems. Ray appeared to have this expertise and we formed a partnership.

At this stage he was a Higher Executive Officer (HEO) and I was the next grade up – Senior Executive Officer (SEO) – but acting up as a Grade 7. He had the ability to see both the big picture and the detail, but he wasn't able to work the politics of the system. So I dealt with the rest of the world, and I could trust him to give me sensible things to say. The relationship, the project and our careers all flourished.

We kept getting into situations where we needed to lean on each other. In time we made this a more explicit mentoring relationship: we sat down and advised each other. We became nervous about being separated, though at times we were in separate commands, and I spent six months working in HR. However, the relationship continued. Every time Ray has been promoted, we have had a period where he has had some explicit mentoring. For example when he became a Grade 6 (the first Senior Management grade, with a secretary and all the trimmings) he had a crisis about how you operate at that level – how you get away from the detail, and remain confident that things will still happen; how you handle the politics. We identified competences like persuasion and negotiation that he had not developed. Up until then he had relied on the force of the argument. I helped him reflect on what being a Grade 6 meant. I made sure that I didn't just give him the things that I do, because we are so different, but we concentrated on the things that are essential for the job.

Now we are both Grade 5s, and I am the Chairman and he is the Managing Director of the Information Systems Branch (ISB). When he became a Grade 5, he had to do more presentations at conferences, and he has found it difficult to enjoy and use these occasions. I have helped him use networking as a major asset in this position.

The mentoring relationship has helped me when we have had some really difficult decisions to make, for example over market testing. Would I lead the bid? What if we lost? We examined different scenarios and how we felt. It became clear that I didn't have a role in the detailed planning. Ray was able to be very explicit about what my role was. He said, without any hesitation, that I had to be the figurehead, the leader who people know and will follow; I had to do the visionary things, go and be seen, listen to the staff, and handle partnerships and competition.

One thing about this relationship is that it is fun. With Ray it is really good, and we have both benefited in our careers and in doing our jobs better. It is difficult to know whether it is a friendship or a working relationship. We have great arguments when we are under pressure, which worry people outside. But the strength of ISB during market testing was the Allen/Hinchcliffe relationship – understanding each others' thinking made us almost unbeatable.

Because we both got such a lot out of this, we realized that we needed other people, so we now look at and work with our skills and preferences and those of our two colleagues in the management team. In turn, we spend quite a lot of time discussing the performance of others and what to do about it, so we have ended up helping others.

Then we became involved in the Hybrid Manager course (an MSc in Information Technology and Management at Sheffield Hallam University), and I started reading about mentoring and making it a formal arrangement for people doing the course part-time. We were very aware of the differences between people and the strengths of others that they could use. Mentoring would not have developed had we not talked about people a lot.

The Hybrid programme made me think about mentoring and we discussed it a lot. Up until then I had not realized the power of hierarchy, how there seemed to be no option if a senior boss suggested it. We have now raised the issue of blame-free divorce. The chapter on male/female relationships in *Everyone Needs a Mentor* (Clutterbuck 1992) was deeply worrying. What was worrying was that I hadn't thought about it. Before that, the decision on choice of mentor was very loose, and this raised the importance of not taking a power position.

We have learned the importance of taking a contractual position. Before, with Ray, it hadn't seemed necessary. Sometimes with the Hybrid managers we seemed to get on all right. You could allow a long period to get to know each other and gradually adjust. With others, if you lack that rapport, you need a definition of what you will do, and a process for agreeing this.

It has helped having training sessions with other mentors at the University. I started without an understanding of how to help people on the course. Now part of what I do is provide the context. They often come with their thoughts about an assignment, and I offer the wider picture. I draw this on the electronic whiteboard and some of them take a print-off and find this helpful. Others seem to want more specific help – references, reports, a look at the structure of what they are doing. They all get a good insight of what it is like to have the wider perspective from the top of the pyramid. Ray is also doing the course, so I act formally as his mentor for this.

I have also mentored a woman not on the course. I have taken a fatherly interest in her career. Occasionally, I set out my problem to her and ask her what she thinks. It helps me and it helps her. I highlight how my job is not easy – perhaps that's why I do it! I do it with management issues for her, and with more technical issues for the Hybrids.

With one of the Hybrids, who was a project manager of the old school – 'this is mine, this is yours' – Ray and I have both mentored him. He has changed enormously. He has built a support relationship in his team. It has worked and it has had an effect on other teams too. They have the makings of a really high performance team.

Another benefit of mentoring to the organization came from the fact that we were early to delayer. Status shouldn't come from position, but the people I mentor have helped me to realize how many landmarks we have taken away. So, we have had to give them a better compass. Mentoring is an important part of that. I have learned a lot about my organization from the people I mentor.

Discussion

Natural to formal. One of the reasons that the formal mentoring scheme in ISB works so well is that the two senior managers both have a strong, positive experience of natural mentoring on which to build. They have used the training opportunities offered by the university to help them hone their skills and fit the way they approach mentoring to the particular task of the formal scheme.

Mutual. Long-term mentoring soon seems to become mutual, and in this case the relationship between Mike and Ray has been highly beneficial to both of their careers and to the work of the branch.

Transitions. Mike noticed how Ray particularly needed mentoring when he was making certain key transitions, such as becoming a senior manager. He was able to focus his effort on these transitions, while avoiding the trap of imposing on Ray his perspective of what that transition had meant to him.

Mentoring in a delayered organization. The metaphor of navigation is a powerful one: delayering takes away a lot of the landmarks, so individuals need their own compasses. Mentoring helps them to get this sense of being able, self-sufficiently, to chart their own course.

Multiple mentoring. Mike is as busy as most senior managers, yet he still has time to mentor several staff. Perhaps this is because he does not see mentoring as additional to his other management tasks, but integral to them.

Friendship and fun. There is no mistaking that Mike finds a lot of friendship and fun in his working life, and mentoring is part of the context that makes this possible.

Reference

Clutterbuck, D (1992) *Everyone Needs a Mentor*, IPM, London, 2nd Edition.

7. MENTOR TO EX-EMPLOYEES: FRANK LORD

Interviewed by David Megginson

Until his recent promotion within the Appleyard Group, Frank Lord was managing director of Appleyards of Chesterfield, a Peugeot dealership that he had established on a new site for the company in 1989.

Frank has a powerful commitment to development, which is manifested in his setting up the Appleyard Learning and Education Centre (ALEC). ALEC obtained a National Training Award (NTA), with the NTA Patron's special commendation for encouraging self-development. Frank was also Chair of Chesterfield Training and Enterprise Council and has been a witness to a parliamentary enquiry into employee development schemes.

He not only coaches his own direct reports, he also mentors many members of staff throughout his organization. Furthermore, he has continued to act as a mentor for people who no longer work with him.

One of the potential problems about being a committed developer is that some of the people whom you help will grow out of the roles that are available in the organization. This has happened on a number of occasions to Frank.

Rather than seeing this as an inevitable cost of a commitment to development, Frank has continued to support, through a mentoring relationship, a number of people who left him to move on to bigger jobs.

Frank's model for mentoring is a simple one. He recalls the process with the acronym 'ARAFAB'. This stands for:

☐ Accomplishment in all that you do, which comes from

☐ Results that you achieve, which are built on your own

☐ Action, which is fuelled by

☐ Feelings, that generate movement, deriving from

☐ Attitudes, which each of us hold, based on our

☐ Beliefs, which need to be thought through.

A positive example of this process is Peter Portlock, who used to work for Frank as a used car sales manager. He wanted to become a general sales manager. There was no opening in Frank's organization, and Peter had concerns about whether he was ready for the transition. Frank told him he thought he had the aptitude, but he was concerned about whether Peter would get the coaching he needed to develop his skills.

When Peter did get his general sales manager job he came back to talk with Frank about difficulties he was having in building a team in his department. Frank took him through the process of thinking deeply about his feelings, attitudes and beliefs, and this had the very practical consequence of helping Peter to recognize that he had to address issues of teamwork company wide.

Peter has kept in touch, and whenever he goes for a job he telephones Frank. He doesn't get solutions from Frank, but questions that encourage him to seek out his own way rigorously.

Sometimes ex-employees contact Frank and say that they are demotivated by the regime they are working in under their new boss. Compared with how it was with Frank, they say that work does not feel right, there is no fun to it. In exploring feelings, attitudes and beliefs, Frank encourages his ex-employees to think broadly about the whole of their lives – business and home. Often this brings out non-work worries that are draining energy away from work performance. Then he returns to the issues at work and encourages his learner to be responsible for creating their feelings from within. Rather than being unduly influenced by the external environment, Frank challenges them to create their own influencing factors, to generate their own feelings. Only then does he turn the conversation to the specific issues about how to win this or that account, how to achieve next month's target.

His message is 'don't add your own negatives to someone else's, don't miss your budget month after month because of the way you are being treated, but create your own feelings and then go for what you know you can achieve'. Frank's reward is when people ring him back, and say that they are grateful for his concern, and that they have gone for it and are achieving again.

Discussion

Mentoring ex-employees. Frank does this because, for him, development and love of people are deeply held values which he encourages others to find for themselves.

Mentor payoffs. Frank mentors ex-employees because it is a worthwhile activity in itself, and one from which he derives great satisfaction. For other people, it may be that networking and having long-term feedback on the impact of their development efforts could also be benefits.

Holistic approach. Frank deals with feelings as well as action, home as well as work, and support as well as tough challenge.

8. CAREER DEVELOPMENT OF A MULTIPLE MENTEE: STEVE RICK

Interviewed by David Megginson

In 1978 I was a plumber with a small family-owned construction company. It employed about 200 people and I worked on a site in Hemel Hempstead. Being inquisitive, I learnt how to use a theo-dolite and a level and in the absence of the site manager became site engineer. One day in the winter of 1978, the managing director, Douglas Peters, turned up on site. He was an Arts graduate from Oxford – an unlikely character to be the managing director of a building company. He came into the site hut and we got talking about my career. At that point my main aspiration was to stay employed, and beyond that I really hadn't given it an awful lot of thought.

I was 24. I had married several months earlier, and the MD suggested that I should give my future a bit more thought. Over the next few weeks that's exactly what I did, think about my career! He came back to the site some weeks later and said that he had decided that the company had reached a size where they needed a personnel officer and he wanted me to consider it. They were already doing some work with the Construction Industry Training Board (CITB) and sharing a group training adviser with three other construction companies. However, with the Employment Protection Act being enforced the following year, there was a whole raft of things that hadn't happened up to now (for example, ensuring that everyone had a contract of employment), which they could no longer ignore. I didn't know what personnel officers did, but jokingly said: 'If it means I get to work in an office as opposed to working on site, I'll do it'. I then made contact with a lot of companies that I thought were big enough to have personnel officers, and I asked if I could meet them, and find out what they did.

The MD opened the door for me, but without really giving too much of a steer. He had already suggested I make an appointment to see him in about ten days time to take our discussions further. When we met, I told him that I had given his suggestion serious thought and been to see quite a few people, had got a broad idea of what personnel involved and believed I could do it. I was getting excited by the whole thing, and quite fortuitously one evening, I was talking to a friend, Julian Gell, who asked what I was up to. When I explained my quest to make sense of personnel, his response was simple: 'Why didn't you say so earlier?' It transpired that he was the remuneration and benefits manager for Kodak: I had not made the connection that this was personnel!

He then sat down with me and helped organize my thoughts. In fact, it was the beginning of two simultaneous mentoring relationships, the MD and my friend from Kodak. It was genuinely a mentoring exercise as I see it, in as much as I was not being given an answer but rather posed some tough, searching questions. Whether that was the intention or not, I don't know, but I saw it very much that way. With hindsight, I saw the development of the relationship with both of them as being similar to that of an athlete and their coach. The coach knows what is possible yet doesn't actually run the race.

I went back to see the MD with a pretty clear idea of what the possibilities might be. I had seen a lot of personnel people in different organizations although I wasn't actually inspired by what I had seen. So I thought 'Yeah, I can do that', perhaps with hindsight, somewhat arrogantly or precociously. I think Douglas was encouraged by what I had done. However, before confirming my appointment he wanted me to meet the chairman, and 'before meeting him there is a book I would like you to read'. He gave me Robert Townsend's book *Up the Organisation*, which debunks the whole idea of having personnel people. I guess that set the tone for both the meeting with the chairman and how I have viewed HR ever since.

In many ways Douglas Peters has had a profound effect on my career, in more ways than he appreciated at the time. I went back and met the chairman and the MD. As I remember it to this day, they were delightful, and I was quite gauche; however, they gave me the job. On the first day in my new job, and to my astonishment, the MD said, 'You will only have this job for two years and then you will need to move on somewhere else, because you will outgrow it'. It was a mind-blowing start to my new career.

Without realizing it at the time both Douglas and Julian gave me my first taste of mentoring relationships.

I left that job after just over two years and was actually head-hunted (although I didn't realize it at the time) by a larger construction company. At the time I had two job offers; one from the CITB. It was the mentoring MD, Douglas Peters, who posed the right questions to me, which helped in deciding my next career move. In the new company, I embarked on another mentoring relationship that was totally different. This was with David Pye who was the training manager; I was appointed as senior training officer.

He was extremely critical, a stickler for detail, yet enormously creative and I learnt a lot from working with him. The mentoring relationship was one where he took some pains, and I think they were deliberate pains, to point out my shortcomings. He was relentless in making me realize that it was not enough to be energetic. To be competent and capable required something else.

I'll always remember my very first appraisal with him. I thought it was grossly unfair. I remember going away from that feeling that I had been humiliated. David chose not to be particularly empathic with me, nor did he work hard at maintaining my self-esteem. He took me to the cleaners over some pretty minor things. However, it's these issues that have stayed with me; the way I expressed myself, the way I put papers together, the need not only to do the right things but to do them right. He instilled in me a sense of order, a sense of standards and the need to influence those in positions of power.

Although he was my line manager, he took a personal interest in what I was doing, which went beyond pure supervision or coaching.

I shall always remember when the company went into divisionalization, and appointed a personnel manager for one of the new divisions. I met the new PM for the first time in the staff canteen, where my boss and colleagues were having lunch with him. I spent some time talking with the PM, and when he left to go to another appointment, I turned to my boss and said, 'So what the hell has he got that I haven't got? Why has he been appointed, why wasn't I considered for the job?' Two months earlier I had been eulogized by the chief executive for special praise in front of the assembled masses for a project in which I had been involved. My critical mentor said, 'Look at his business card. What does it say?' The new personnel manager had his name and 'BA, MIPM'. My mentor-boss's response was 'What have you got?' He was right. I had absolutely nothing, other than a catalogue of experience. I resolved from that moment onwards that I would never be in that position again. David knew what he was doing.

This mentor would be what I would recognize today as an excellent training manager. He had spent a lot of time in the Construction Industry Training Board since its inception and had had some wonderful exposure to all sorts of training and development approaches. I learned a heck of a lot from working with him, but the dream did not last – we were all made redundant as the company unwisely diversified into non-core activities.

I got a job with another building company for a short time just to pay the mortgage. I left them after a year to go into local government where I got into my next mentoring relationship with Chris Hutton who was first of all my boss, but also became a close friend. He was running what was called a development team, which was essentially a small occupational psychology unit within the local authority, which suited him as he had recently finished his PhD. Working with Chris was a permanent tutorial.

The relationship was one where he would never give me an answer to anything. If I said, 'Well how should we do this?' his response was always 'What do you think? What do you feel is right? What do your senses tell you?' I learned from this relationship about the capabilities that individuals have if they only dig deep enough, and that was enormously valuable. Working with Chris was fairly traumatic, for he was always skating on the thin edges of legitimacy in the working environment, testing himself and others continuously.

The local authority sponsored me to go off and do a Diploma in Management Studies (DMS) which I did concurrently with my degree, and at the same time I also completed the IPM graduateship examinations.

Working with my new boss helped me explore a whole range of other options, particularly in the area of group dynamics so that during the DMS, together with a number of other students, we essentially took control of the course and got the tutorial group to experiment, which included clubbing together to get the Tavistock Institute to come and work with us as a learning group.

Chris and I were peers in many respects, yet it was he who unlocked so much by getting me to think 'outside the box'.

By now I was able to go into meetings and not have a solution or answers. I clearly remember going into my very first management team session, to talk to a group of managers about the development of their subordinates. After listening to their discussions, I was able to say, 'I don't think it's your subordinates that are the problem; I've seen the enemy and it is you'. A couple of years earlier I would have felt obliged to have a training solution. Chris has continued to be a sounding board, and someone I talk to about relationships and issues confronting me, even now.

I left local government in 1987 and really didn't have any kind of mentoring relationship until about 1989/90, when I was a student of David Guest at the London School of Economics. David supervised my thesis for my Masters Degree and again he was very much like my previous mentor, very challenging. I always had to work hard, because he posed the tough questions. It's this notion of posing the challenging question, such as 'What is your unique perspective on this? I don't want to have the perspective of Ed Schein or Chris Argyris or Tom Peters. I want your views and analysis'.

David asked fundamental, searching questions and I valued him for that as well as for being an outstanding teacher. I rate my time as a student with him as a watershed. I realized for the first time what was happening and I started being able to work with that understanding. It was very powerful, extremely powerful. Essentially, it was the notion that no-one else has the answers – it's up to you, but it helps if someone is posing the questions.

I continue to talk to David, and probably four or five times a year we meet and discuss issues of common interest, to the point where we have worked together as peers/collaborators. David has seen how my ideas have developed and has been enormously supportive. He also has encouraged me to think outside the box.

I joined ICL in 1990, and my very first assignment was with the finance director, John Lillywhite. He and I became co-conspirators on a number of projects to radically change the nature and shape of the business.

He was very much a mentor and not my line boss. Before I accepted my present job at the Royal Bank, I actually went to talk to John before I talked to my line boss. I have so much respect for him because he was most unusual for a finance director in that he was equally interested in *how* business was conducted as much as what was conducted. He said to me when I was considering moving to the Bank, 'I think it's an opportunity for you. You've got a precious talent so be careful how you use it, don't waste it.' He made me stop and think for the first time that I do actually have some abilities. I had up to this point thought my career to date had been a result of good luck. However, he was both generous – and specific – in his feedback.

Generosity in observation is something I tend to reject unless it's well grounded, and it's from someone who I know is being totally sincere.

John observed that I was prepared to go into the unknown and take risks, personal risks; and be committed, and not then walk away when things got hot or started to go wrong. An example he gave – he invited me into Ireland because he didn't know what the problem was, and he believed that in half an hour I'd got right to the point. We changed what had started as a business planning event into a total reappraisal of the entire strategy for our businesses in Ireland. This resulted in us recruiting a new managing director.

In the change programme we ran at ICL, he also valued the fact that I worried about it. I think he made me realize how important it is that you do have to take ownership and have a clear vision of where you are trying to get to, and how important ownership is in making things happen. The example he gave was that having me around 'was like having a stone in your shoe, you kept coming round prodding, and asking the difficult questions'. He believed this role was important, and if we hadn't had that, we wouldn't have gone from 1000 people to 14 in two-and-a-half years at the UK headquarters. John was extremely generous in both thought and deed.

I still ring him now and again and we talk about how to make things happen. It's never just a conversation, it's usually about influencing at the top, how to keep people 'on side'. John taught me the art of strategic selling of organizational change, looking at it as a series of sales that have to be made to a number of stakeholders. This was reinforced by my many friends among the sales force, particularly Jim Devlin, who used the strategic sales funnel to devastating effect particularly when managing change and in his own career development.

John lived through the period when ICL almost went out of business. His parents died when he was very young and he was very much the lad who joined as the commercial apprentice and worked his way up. Yet he still had this openness, respect and wonderful welcoming of new ideas, and the grace and liberty to embrace them.

I also see David Megginson as a mentor. I have been a client and he has been the consultant. I have had many client/consultant relationships before where the consultant will give you what they think you want, but David has been quite candid with me on a number of occasions about myself, my behaviour, and the way I conduct myself. This has made me stop to think, and I value that as an igniter of ideas and thought. I value David as a friend now, but I still think that I get value out of a whole range of discussions. I'm unsure where the threshold or boundaries between mentoring, managing and friendship are any more.

David asks questions in different ways. We had a conversation in my car going down the M3 and it made me stop – it was not an obvious question like, 'Why the hell are you doing that', it was almost dismissive. I think it was where I was going into 'auto rant' about someone in ICL and it was his basic sense of orientation towards humanism that said, 'How is he feeling about you, and why is he feeling that?' David was asking questions in a slightly different but nevertheless quite challenging way, although they may not have been obvious questions to anyone else who was listening at the time. However, for me they were powerful, and I picked them up as fundamental questions about the way I behave, operate and communicate.

I think it would be remiss of me to leave this topic without mentioning another person, Neville Bunn, with whom I have had a mentoring relationship since 1990. When I joined ICL he was the head of graduate recruitment and development and I was ap-pointed as management development manager. We were peers. Within six months I was promoted to be his boss. Neville has proved to be not only an enormous supporter and friend, but someone whose opinion I value enormously. He was 52 when I first started working with him. Neville had been there, seen it, done it, made the film and written the book. He had three very talented sons of his own, who were younger than myself, but nevertheless, he was a bit of an uncle/father figure in many respects. It's an interesting relationship when you have someone who is very talented, who is older than you, yet is working as your subordinate.

I used to get terribly frustrated with some situations and people at ICL. On innumerable occasions he was able to help me sit down and think through to a reasoned solution. I valued his patience and the insight he had into my psyche. Neville acted very much as a sounding board and I used to sometimes say, half-jokingly, that if he ever got fed up with his day job, he could be a fabulous editor, he used to de-tune a lot of the more aggressive papers that I would churn out in a stream of consciousness. Equally he would spend hours just talking to me, letting me talk through issues and problems as I saw them, because in an HQ role there were a lot of highly sensitive issues – there was no one else I could talk to.

I trusted him implicitly, and I valued his contribution in terms of helping me work through issues and problems. He often did this not by asking questions, but very much by listening and letting me work through, almost letting me exercise the Socratic process of talking. I think I learned a lot by just having to articulate my point of view. He was very good at creating the space and environment for me to do that. He was a very thoughtful man, a man of great ability, and much loved human being, within the ICL family. He is now retired from ICL.

I have since employed Neville as a consultant at the Bank, and he is now acting as a formal mentor to one of our young managers who is taking responsibility for graduate recruitment. I think she is learning a tremendous amount from him. He makes learning very enjoyable and I think that is important as well.

On being a mentor

Mentors are people who are very thoughtful and unselfish in their observations. They are very generous in their time and there is no hidden agenda.

My mentors have been sounding boards, but also very careful sounding boards, very much thinking through what can happen and how – that seems to be important. They have in all cases applied the practice of reflection as a key ingredient of the relationship.

On being a learner

One of the things I am conscious of in this conversation is that being a learner in the mentoring relationship can be quite selfish. It's very self-centred, almost egocentric, not unlike that of an athlete and coach, or indeed potentially like a parent and child.

I suppose what makes it work with me is partly that I have a basic insecurity and lack of confidence in my abilities, and I need reassurance. Also I value the people who have had deep experiences themselves, been through trauma and difficult situations, major changes, and have a perspective. It's interesting that if you look at the people who I consider to have been mentors, they have all gone through that.

Again, I have found the help of mentors particularly significant, having been written off as a youngster. I've always maintained that the worst thing that anyone can ever say is that you'll never amount to anything or you'll never achieve a particular goal or target.

I don't consciously go out to seek mentors. However, there are people I meet at various stages of my life whose opinions, thoughts and ideas I value, even though they may not entirely concur with my own. They can be a boss, subordinate, peer or friend. The relationship can last a matter of days or span a number of years. It may be situational or not, however, in my experience, the relationship is seldom formal.

Discussion

Qualities of mentee. Steve is restless and ambitious, wanting to take opportunities himself, and responding to anyone who creates them for him. He tunes into people who are on the same wavelength; it is the long wave, which addresses the large and wide processes in an individual's or an organization's life.

Qualities of mentor. For this kind of learner the style of the mentor does not seem to matter too much. What makes a difference is whether they are able to put the learner into some challenging situations. An attention to the whole person and having an eye on where they might be going does seem to be crucial, however. The most consistently useful skill seems to be to ask the questions that penetrate to the heart of the issues that the mentee is facing, and this requires a capacity for empathy and an imaginative understanding of the other's position. Also a depth of personal experience seems to be important in the mentor.

Basis for the relationship. This case seems to offer a string of relationships, some of which are in the style of the early ones cited in the US literature – someone being picked out and given exceptional opportunities because they have an exceptional amount to offer. What I also notice in these relationships is a strong sense of generosity – that the learner will not remain for ever, and the deed is not done for the rewards that the individual or the company might gain, but because it is right in itself.

Learner-led, diffused relationships. This case provides a model for learners taking responsibility for assembling the help that they need, and finding it from a number of sources.

Reference

Townsend, R (1970) *Up the Organization*, Michael Joseph, London.

9. CHIEF EXECUTIVE WITH A BLACK MANAGER: STEVE CLOSE WITH JASBIR BANGERH

Steve Close Director of Chantry Housing Association, Wakefield, mentors Jasbir Bangerh on the Management Training Initiative (MTI) for the Charitable Trust of Housing Associations in West Yorkshire (CTHAWY).

Interviewed by David Megginson

The MTI is designed to attract able and experienced Black staff who aspire to become middle and senior managers within the social housing sector. It appoints trainees to one placement of 18 months or two of nine months each. At the end of this period there is no guarantee of a permanent appointment, but the scheme aims for 80 per cent of participants to achieve permanent employment in senior or principal officer posts within six months of the end of the scheme.

Jasbir Bangerh was appointed to Chantry Housing Association (HA) initially for nine months, although she subsequently agreed to remain in Chantry HA for the full 18 months. She was appointed to the role of personnel and training manager – a position that had not existed at Chantry HA before.

Steve says Chantry became involved with the MTI out of a concern for equal opportunities, and a recognition that Black people were under-represented at senior management level. Jasbir quips that it also gave them a personnel manager on the cheap; however, this was not part of the original plan, indeed the role for the trainee was originally going to be in another function.

Jasbir is the only MTI trainee mentored by the chief executive of the employer, and this had advantages for her in having access to the strategic thinking of top management. Potential disadvantages, such as difficulty of access and resentment of colleagues, were not seen as major problems in the open management culture at Chantry.

Jasbir is clear that Steve's commitment to her individual development, as well as getting objectives achieved, has been the essential feature in enabling Steve fill the role of both line manager and mentor without role conflict. Steve says that he gives Jaz more time than permanent members of his team, and that they set development targets as well as performance targets. They have regular meetings to review progress, and knock a hole in barriers. He thinks the other managers might find such a regime oppressive, but in Jaz's case the role was a fair quantum leap in her experience, and she valued this support.

When they first started working together, Jasbir was apprehensive about what her boss was going to be like, because of a previous bad experience. However, as it turned out, it was really easy: in their first meeting Steve told her some sensitive, confidential stuff, which really helped and left her feeling that it was going to work. A habit of mutual honesty developed from this meeting.

He often gave her tasks without specifying what she needed to find out – to encourage her to think through the issues. As he had designed the personnel practices that had been established at Chantry, he felt it was pointless giving Jaz his ideas – it was his ideas he wanted her to improve upon! Jaz felt that Steve's willingness to let go of control and ownership helped her development enormously.

Objective setting was built into the scheme, and, for the first six months, they met weekly to review what Jaz had achieved, what she had learned, the blockages she had encountered and what she was to do next week.

They also set larger-scale objectives, which were reviewed bimonthly. Steve felt that his keenness to get things cracked and Jaz's willingness to have a go at whatever he gave her led to their setting over-optimistic goals initially. Jaz took the initiative in cutting these back, once the reality of involvement in the MTI scheme and doing a professional course (Institute of Personnel Development – IPD) came home to them.

Jaz was also supported by the MTI project manager and by a Black counsellor, appointed by the project available for the trainees. Jasbir valued Steve's encouragement of flexible working – going out to visit other organizations from which they might learn, working from home if necessary, prioritizing attendance at MTI monthly meetings, attending the IPD course, and, crucially, having a say in the projects she was to do and how to go about them. Steve was clear that the scheme was more than a job, it was about developing an individual.

When necessary they talk about personal issues, and this they feel makes you a human being to the other, but primarily their relationship could be described as intensely professional and professionally intense.

Jaz received some challenges early on about decisions she had made, which had perhaps been influenced by a perception by others that she was getting special treatment; however, she saw this as quite healthy, and was helped by being able to talk the issues through and find solutions with her mentor. She always came out enthused from her meetings with Steve.

She did not, however, always get her way and Steve has been able to exercise his line-manager role in rejecting some of her proposals. The fact that he listens fully to them, and respects her view, helps overcome the potential conflict between line and mentor roles.

She gets from the relationship access to the top management perspective, and time to think through and come to terms with challenges faced by her work during this concentrated period of development. Steve, as mentor, gets an opportunity to have someone going beyond his own vision for a particular area of the organization's work, and the organization gets some accelerated progress on one area of its activity and a model of how to manage an intensely developmental relationship.

When I observed their meetings we noticed the following about how Steve went about his mentoring:

☐ he makes a great many proposals about what Jaz could do (22 per cent of everything he says is a proposal). She finds this useful, especially as he is usually open to alternative suggestions

☐ he constantly checks that he has understood what Jaz says (15 per cent testing understanding). She finds this helpful, as she feels she is not always clear in her verbal communication, and this helps her to think again and clarify what she meant

☐ he seems not to disagree at all – his strongest disagreement in a meeting lasting nearly two hours was in the form of a statement 'I am not sure it should be...'. He does express his views but he does this by making proposals or giving information about his internal states, thoughts and feelings (giving internal information 14 per cent)

☐ he gives the background to his thinking about policy and management practices

☐ he supports Jaz and encourages her to get what she wants from other departments of Chantry, and in terms of pursuing her own development. He also expresses concern for her development as a person, for example about how she balances work and leisure

☐ he is empathic of others, suggesting how they might see a situation

☐ he gives candid views about the organizations that Jaz may come into contact with, because he wants the best interests of Chantry and Jaz's own future to be served. They recognized that this might prejudice Jaz's views about the organization, but both think, on balance, that Steve's offering these opinions is helpful

☐ he encourages her to value her own experience and to recognize what she has done, and how she has developed.

Discussion

Combining line and mentor role. This is done effectively because of the high degree of awareness that both parties have of the nature of their relationship. It is also helped in this case that Jaz is not a permanent member of staff, but is on a scheme which has a finite time span.

Chief Executive as mentor. This works very well, as it gives the learner a strategic perspective. Steve's open style prevents any difficulties for Jaz or other staff at Chantry.

Cycles of meetings. This relationship is run on a relatively regular series of meetings. This is not seen as bureaucratic or restrictive, again perhaps because of the time-bounded nature of the scheme.

Mentoring for diversity. The scheme provides for the development of ethnic minority members into middle management positions. This does not seem to produce problems of envy for others in the culture of a housing association like Chantry.

PART 4
So What and Now What?

4
APPLYING THE LESSONS

INTRODUCTION

In our concluding chapter we ask what our experience and the examples in the rest of this book tell us about mentoring schemes and mentoring relationships. We will put these findings in the context of the changing world of work, and explore why mentoring is, *par excellence*, an approach for development that is right for the times. Finally we look speculatively into the future and address the question of where mentoring seems to be heading.

Mentoring – not an end in itself

As we have talked and listened with many mentors and learners over the years, it has become increasingly clear that mentoring is a step on the journey of development, rather than the destination.

From the foundation of the Training Boards in the 1960s, training departments increasingly attempted to appropriate responsibility for learning in organizations. The message was that learning took place on courses, and that the training department was responsible for access to, and indeed often the budgets, design and delivery of, these precious experiences.

In recent years there has been pressure to increase the involvement of the line manager in these processes. Three of the pressures that have contributed to this trend are:

☐ cuts in the staffing of large central training establishments

☐ outsourcing of many previously centralized services

☐   the devolution of cost and profit responsibility to smaller and smaller units.

Each of these changes in the organizational context has made it less feasible to have training or HRD departments responsible for the management of learning. However, none of these changes has actually made it any easier for line managers to take on this role. In fact managers themselves, like training departments, are under increasing time and cost pressure to restrict their development activities. In our view, there is still some way to run with the trend of increasing line manager responsibility. The case for this development is explored in a forthcoming book edited by Stephen Gibb and David Megginson — *Managers as Developers*. The conclusion of this set of readings by leaders in the field is that this trend is growing, but not without putting considerable and, at times, illegitimate pressure on managers as developers.

A trend now emerging is the contribution that can be made by mentors. Clearly, mentors too are under increasing pressure. However, the mentor's role is different from the manager as developer in that while mentors are doing their mentoring, they usually do not have any other agendas with the person that they are helping: they are just there to develop their learner.

While one of the authors of this book was finishing this last chapter under tight deadlines he had an appointment for a mentoring session. At the end the learner apologized for keeping him so long, but the mentor had been oblivious of the time during the session. Afterwards it was easy to say, 'Should I have allocated those four hours in that way?' While it was going on, time seemed to stand still. Many of the individuals whom we have contacted in our work and in getting the accounts in this book seem to find the same. Mentoring is indeed an absorbing and rewarding process.

There is another sense in which mentoring can be seen as a continuation of the development from HRD to line manager responsibility. With this perspective we can view the transition in terms of an increasing responsibility on the part of learners themselves to manage their own development. If the evolution of responsibility for learning in organizations is seen in this way, then we can see that the move from the 'granny' training department to the 'granny' manager may not have been such a large step. However, as the stories in this book attest, a key feature of the mentor's role is precisely that they let the learner make the running, manage the relationship and take the decisions. In this way, mentoring takes us a substantial step further along the journey to individuals taking responsibility for their own learning.

Of course, as we said earlier, mentoring is not the end of the journey. We would envisage that following the surge of interest in mentoring there will be a greater emphasis on helping everyone in organizations to be responsible for pulling together all the resources and help that they need to develop themselves. Figure 1 illustrates this process.

HRD department ⟶ Line manager ⟶ Mentor ⟶ Learners themselves

Figure 1 *The evolution of responsibility for development*

We turn now to the lessons that can be drawn directly from the stories and life histories, the schemes and programmes which we have included in this book. First we look at the lessons which emerge from the organizations and schemes described in Part 2. The cases are referred to by the name of the organization, so that you can make easy reference to them if there are aspects that particularly engage your interest. The individual cases, which we will explore later, are referred to by the name of the mentor and or the learner.

We bring together issues that we identified while preparing or reviewing these cases. Sometimes the evidence from the cases all seems to point in the same direction. With other themes, the stories may appear to contradict each other. For these issues, it may be that there is not a clear prescription that can be made about how to deal with this aspect of mentoring. This finding, in itself, may be very useful for practitioners, however. For example, we had previously thought that it was best if the mentor was substantially more senior than the learner, but not too much more senior! On the basis of the range of experience that we have here, it seems that all manner of differences in seniority can work perfectly well. This is an important finding, because it means that scheme organizers defining the boundaries, or individuals choosing a mentoring partner, can free themselves from the restrictions that we might previously have applied, and recognize the support for the notion of choosing the one who seems right, regardless of formal status.

In other cases where the individual stories appear to point to different conclusions, it may be that there is some deeper, further factor that provides an underlying order to the apparent but superficial conflict in the data. For example, it is often said that line managers should not take on the role of mentor. In these cases, too, we have one or two examples of line managers having a hard time resolving the conflict between the two roles. Alternatively, learners might find the two contributions hard to accept from the same person. However, we have other examples where both mentor and learner have handled the dual role gracefully and effectively. With this theme we are drawn to the conclusion that the underlying factor is the level of awareness of the parties involved. If both of them are interpersonally skilled, and this means conscious of the impact of their own interpersonal processes, then the possible conflicts of role can be triumphantly overcome, and in fact can be used to deepen the learning.

THEMES EMERGING FROM ORGANIZATION CASES

We have put the themes together under the following headings:

- [ ] context of work
- [ ] national culture
- [ ] support and organizational culture
- [ ] aims
- [ ] mutuality
- [ ] diversity
- [ ] training
- [ ] dealing with difficulties
- [ ] network of relationships
- [ ] boundaries and the future of mentoring.

We will deal with each in turn.

Context of work

In Linda Holbeche's financial services organization, the flattened structure was painting a new picture of careers. Rather than progression, the new considerations, which mentoring was designed to help, concerned employability and making the most of the present job and project opportunities. This new organization also meant that they had to consider peer mentoring, as there were fewer senior people to call upon.

One radical and remarkable solution to this problem of the shortage of mentors is provided by Jöran Hultman's story of Svenska Nestlé. Here they used 70-year old, retired business people as the mentors, with very positive results.

National cultures

The example from Sweden of using retired mentors raises questions of how sharp national differences might be. The respect for the wisdom of old age differs widely between countries, and it may be that such a strategy may be less acceptable in Britain with its emphasis on youth, and a policy of retiring people at earlier and earlier ages.

Liz Borredon's story from France again raises questions of national difference. She experiences the French culture of formality and power distance as militating against the development of close personal relationships between hierarchically distinct roles.

This raises interesting implications for international companies. Almost certainly it is not appropriate to produce a uniform scheme to be applied across national boundaries. The relationships will just be interpreted differently in different cultures.

Support and organizational culture

Mentoring seems to work best when it is going with the grain of other initiatives in the organization. For example, Lewisham's senior management supported equal opportunities in general, so the mentoring scheme for Black managers gained their wholehearted commitment, and this was crucial to its success. In Asda, Oxford RHA and ICL the same lessons apply. This is further supported by Bob Garvey's negative example of Engineering UK, where senior management's actions belied their words, and this contributed to the failure of the scheme.

Aims

Clarity of aims has long been held as an important design principle for mentoring schemes. Our data supports this view, with Norman McLean's National Mentoring Consortium case providing a good example. The negative story of Engineering UK again supports this view. This scheme was asked to carry too much, and it broke in the attempt.

The range of aims is widespread, from schemes that border on coaching in terms of their specificity in contributing to performance improvement, to the Nestlé case at the other extreme, where wisdom, balance and seeking for purpose were included alongside more workaday concerns.

The Oxford RHA case reminds us that mentoring does not have to be seen just as a hugely long-term affair. If goals are specific and participants are highly motivated, then much can be achieved in a few short meetings. However, this should not be seen as *carte blanche* for using mentoring as a crisis intervention. Usually things do indeed take time, but in the circumstances of a narrow focus and willing participation much can be achieved quite quickly.

The ICL case, which looks forward to the future, is placing a demanding burden on the mentoring relationship, appropriating some of the tasks normally associated with line managers. It will be interesting to see how this works – particularly as ICL Learning Consultancy are also offering this comprehensive mentoring support to all those who work there – not just their full time consultant staff, but part-time associates and contract workers.

Mutuality

Mutual benefits are a recurring theme in mentoring schemes. The BEAT scheme described by Coral Gardiner is a strong example of this, where in spite, or perhaps because, of the huge differences in circumstances between mentors and learners there was widespread report of mutual benefit. The Oxford RHA scheme is another example of this process from an organization-based scheme.

Diversity

One of the powerful ways in which mentoring is used is in fostering diversity and helping to overcome barriers for those disadvantaged in employment. The BEAT scheme shows this process working with the multiple-disadvantaged group of inner city young offenders. Mary Evans' Lewisham case is an example in a local authority, and the National Mentoring Consortium's programme works with Black undergraduates. In this scheme it is interesting to note that at first they relied solely upon Black mentors. Then, as numbers grew, learners were offered the possibility of having White mentors. Some took up this opportunity, and there is an important lesson here about letting participants in the scheme set the pace and make individual choices.

Training

The position of training in these examples is varied. In some schemes, like the Benefits Agency's described by Pam Fricker, it is seen as central, and lots of it is required. In others, a little seems to be enough, as in the case of Oxford RHA and Lewisham, where the learners were keen to get together, but the mentors less so. In yet others there was regret that not enough training had been provided, as in the EDHEC case in France and the Engineering UK example where the scheme eventually failed.

The underlying issue here seems to be the level of support for the initiative and how well it integrates with other activities in the organization. It seems to be the case that the stronger the support and integration, the less training is needed. Regrettably, the less support there is from the top and the less the venture is integrated into other projects, then the more demand there is for training, but the less effect it seems to have. This is another example of training on its own not being enough. A more organizational focus is desirable.

The EDHEC scheme also illustrates, however, that training needs are not always obvious at the launch. Sometimes participants need to get into the process before they can recognize that it is creating needs for their own development.

Dealing with difficulties

EDHEC too illustrates how determination and flexibility can lead to a scheme making a contribution even in circumstances where there is hostility or misunderstanding. Engineering UK lacked the enthusiasts to push the scheme forward and champions to put their hearts into it.

One clear lesson from these examples is the value of piloting or starting with a scheme of modest scope. Lewisham and Asda both adopted this strategy with success, and it was lack of piloting that contributed to the sinking of the Engineering UK scheme.

Network of relationships

Mentoring is part of a web of relationships that can support individuals in organizations. These cases highlight how it is important that mentors work out with line managers and training staff who is responsible for what. In most of the examples this was well done and did not lead to any severe problems.

One principle widely adopted is that all issues of performance and pay have to lie firmly with the line manager. The story of ICL Learning Consultancy is therefore of particular interest because it challenges this consensus.

Boundaries and the future of mentoring

The ICL case points to a future where the line manager will have less say, and where other arrangements will have to be made to carry out the line-manager functions that remain. Mentors, in ICL's view, will have a large part to play in this process. Is mentoring moving into the centre of the web of learning and managing?

The boundaries of the process seem to be extending, at all events. Team mentoring is being talked about, and although we have reservations about using the term mentoring to describe these processes, they certainly share some of the features of mentoring.

Peer mentoring is becoming more widely accepted, and will, we predict, pass into the mainstream in the next few years. External mentoring is already established for groups disadvantaged in employment and for those at the very top of organizations. Will it spread to a wider range of people? If each employee were responsible for managing their personal training budget, how many of them would spend it on getting support from a mentor; and would this be money well spent?

We do not propose to offer definitive answers to these questions, but from our experience of a huge number of schemes blossoming in diverse places, it is clear to us that mentoring is a process whose time has come.

THEMES EMERGING FROM INDIVIDUAL CASES

One of the difficulties in understanding mentoring has been the dearth of live examples of what happens in mentoring relationships. This is perhaps not surprising, given the confidential nature of the relationship, and the deep issues that are often struggled with in this private space. We are fortunate to have had access to the rich and varied store of experience presented in Part 3.

Moving on now to the themes we have identified, we have used another list of headings that overlaps with the one for organizations. This time we look at these issues from the individual's point of view, which can personalize and point up the implications for scheme organizers as well as for individual participants. The issues are:

☐   changing context of work

☐   support

☐   challenge/honesty

☐   change in the helping role

☐   mutuality/gratitude

☐   awareness

☐   diversity

☐   informal to formal

☐ use of external help

☐ major transitions

☐ network of relationships

☐ status differences.

We will deal with each in turn.

Changing context of work

Change is putting more pressure on line managers and making the need for mentors more pressing. This is graphically illustrated in the case of Mike Allen at the Employment Department Information Systems branch. The ordered and well-regulated world in the headquarters of a 'great department of state' has changed. For this rapidly delayering organization a lot of the employment landmarks have been swept away. For many of his staff this is a disconcerting experience. As this stability has broken down, mentors have been seen as providing an important point that the navigators can use to orient themselves in the increasingly troubled waters of organizational life.

Steve Rick, the multiple mentee, has managed huge changes in the organizations he has worked in, and massive development in his own role, with the challenge and support of a series of mentors. His relationship with them has frequently extended beyond the time they were working in the same organization.

Support

Support is often seen as being at the core of the mentoring relationship. Our cases endorse this view. Mike Allen talks about friendship and fun; Frank Lord offers holistic integration of home and work; Steve Rick, tuned into the long wave of life changes gets empathy and imaginative understanding from his multiple mentors. We could go on. These qualities are all too rare in organizations today, and yet mentoring relationships seem to be situations where these rich and rewarding processes can flourish.

Challenge/honesty

Shirley Joan Collie in her mentoring of undergraduate Mohamed Takolia came to recognize that what she did in the mentoring sessions and in between them was at least as important as what she said in the sessions. For someone learning about a new world it was valuable to have a window onto this world, and to have someone who could provide a template of how to behave there. Shirley Joan had to *be* prompt and time conscious and had to demonstrate that she met her commitments to others in order to illustrate these two dimensions of the life of large organizations.

So, challenge comes from how mentors act. It also comes from what they say, and, in particular, how they say it. Steve Rick has had a number of mentors in his fast moving career, from plumber to directorial responsibility in a 'Financial Times 50' company in less than 20 years. He noticed that what his mentors had in common was a way of asking challenging questions – which threw the questions back to him. His mentors were able to spot the points where something was unresolved and to help him focus down upon it, even if it was somewhat uncomfortable. Mentors do not challenge by bullying. They do it by opening up the big questions, not in a generalized and portentous way, but by attending closely to what is going on for the learner and dealing with the demanding issues when they appear.

Change in the helping role

Mentoring relationships often have to change as a result of changed circumstances. Bob Garvey's Jane and John are a fine example of how mentoring relationships have to evolve over time, as in the case of Lesley Martinson. Unforeseen and marked changes in role can lead the most exquisitely crafted development agreement to be largely irrelevant. Mentors can help by modelling the change in gear that is appropriate in the new circumstances. Mike Allen's long mentoring relationship with Ray Hinchcliffe, who is now his peer, is another example of how mentors and learners need to be sensitive to shifting circumstances, and to be able to switch, in Mike's case from helping Ray to build relationships, to tackling promotions, to becoming a senior manager, and then to providing support while Ray studied on his MSc in Management and IT.

Mutuality/gratitude

One of the things that we comment on in our opening chapter is the mutuality of benefit that seems to be a feature of mentoring. These cases confirm this phenomenon. Phill Brown and Catherine Moore, in spite of the considerable distance in seniority and experience between them, were both able to identify benefits for themselves. Phill, in spite of expecting the relationship to be mostly giving on his part, talks of being made to think hard, being refreshed, and giving himself perspective; not a bad crop from a one-way, giving relationship!

Jane Smith and John Jones in Bob Garvey's case found that they were both committed to the relationship and wanted to continue it after John's move. It was only the harshness of the climate in Jane's organization that prevented her from doing this.

The long relationship between Mike Allen and Ray Hinchcliffe is an interesting one, where often in Mike's account it is hard to tell who is being helped and who is helping. The two partners have different capabilities and needs and the relationship is truly symbiotic, and yet at the same time it does not seem to be fostering dependency, but rather to be generating some highly charged relishing of difference.

Generosity is a word that crops up often when people describe mentoring relationships, and it is used explicitly by Steve Rick in his description of the motives he ascribes to several of his mentors.

Awareness

One of the features of mentoring relationships that people we have spoken to value most is this sense of being on another plane from the humdrum or hectic level of the workaday world. At the same time they do not feel remote from this world. They are separate from it and yet in touch with it. This detached engagement seems to be the ideal circumstance for the development of conscious awareness. Such awareness is what enables individuals to see themselves as being able to act freely – to take control of their own destiny, rather than feeling like victims of an oppressive fate.

This gives the mentoring encounter the quality that we have heard described, a bit fancifully for some, as a sacred space. Steve

Close and Jasbir Bangerh have this kind of quality in their relationship. It seems to lie at the root of their ability to make what is both a mentoring and a line relationship flourish.

Diversity

Some mentoring schemes are set up to deal formally with diversity issues, and we have examples here, with Paul as a disabled employee being given assistance by Patricia. Mohamed is a Black undergraduate being helped by Shirley Joan in the National Mentoring Consortium scheme, and Jasbir is a Black junior manager having an opportunity to develop middle management skills and experience with Steve Close's organization.

In addition to this formal dimension, mentoring seems to flourish in circumstances of diversity. Whether it is diversity of experience or temperament or style, the mentoring pairs we have encountered seem to thrive on the differences, as opposed to seeing them as an impediment to empathy and productive closeness.

Informal to formal

Much of the literature on mentoring polarizes around the informal/formal dimension. People either value the natural, spontaneousness of informal associations, based on affinity, or they assert the value of the impersonal, equitable, regulated nature of formal alliances.

Our cases show a much freer interchange between the two poles. Phill Brown had no training from Yorkshire Electricity. He seemed to use his native wit to work out how to develop an appropriate relationship. Patricia's link with Paul started in an informal way, which was initially quite hostile, but which developed into mutual respect. It was only after this had happened that Paul was in the circumstances where he wanted a mentor and at that point he was willing to choose Patricia. Lesley Martinson felt able to choose her own mentor and for that person to be someone junior to herself in rank and age. This highly unusual state of affairs was able to be institutionalized within the scheme in which she was involved. Mike Allen, again, started in a natural bond, which only many years later became part of a programme.

Use of external help

Mentoring archetypically involves two people who sort it out privately between each other, though each may be helped, through training or other means, to improve the way they work together. Again, characteristically, both parties work for the same organization, although there are honourable exceptions to this among schemes to help those groups disadvantaged in employment to gain access to organizations. Both Shirley Joan Collie and Steve Close were involved in such schemes, although in Steve's case it was a half-way-house situation, as Jasbir was assigned his housing association for nine months, and, because the placement worked so well, she eventually stayed for another nine month period.

An interesting example of external help is given in the case described by Bob Garvey. Here his role as supportive researcher enabled him to suggest a way forward when the relationship had come to an impasse.

Two organizational cases—David Clutterbuck's and Mike Green's in the NHS—are examples where an external role, in this case that of the mentors themselves, is necessary. When someone is right at the top of the company, it is often not possible to find anyone able to fulfil the mentor's role from within. In this case being able to seek external help seems not only necessary, but also valuable in opening up new perspectives.

Major transitions

In our definition in Chapter 1 we indicated that we saw mentoring as being about major transitions, and this does seem to be one of the features that differentiates it from most other development methods, whether they are carried out at work or on some separate event. Coaching or courses *might* lead to transforming experiences, but they are seldom set up to do so. In mentoring, a weather eye is kept open for just such possibilities, and as a consequence they tend to crop up rather frequently.

In our sample, Shirley Joan Collie and Phill Brown were helping their learner across the divide between education and work, so the transition was built into the formal specification of the link. Mike

Allen's helping of Ray came to one of those special transitions when Ray made his move across into senior management.

Network of relationships

Richard Caruso, in his brilliant book describing mentoring in Motorola (see Chapter 1), emphasizes that mentoring is best seen as a dispersed learner driven relationship. The point about it being learner-driven has been explored at the start of this chapter and in many of the cases, but the issue of it being dispersed deserves a further word here.

As the old certainties about unity of command and other principles derived from military experience are eroded, the opportunity and the need arise for individuals to collect their own network of helpers to deal with their situation. So we have Mike Allen having a group of learners outside of his direct reports whom he supports; we have Steve Rick collecting a series of mentors over his career, but maintaining contact with them when he moves on; and Frank Lord keeping his networks radically open by sustaining helping links with people who no longer work in his company.

We have also seen the challenges of managing this network, and the importance of treading carefully and thoughtfully in cases like Lesley Martinson's, when she landed up being mentored by someone who reported to someone who reported to her.

Status differences

The most radical relationship we have come across that contradicts the old certainties about the appropriate seniority gap between mentor and learner is that of Lesley Martinson. Many of our examples had major differences in levels, or involved chief executives, and seemed to work well. Others had slight or reverse differences and also flourished! As we said earlier, it is not the status differences but the awareness brought to the relationship that seems to be the factor crucial to success.

THE FUTURE OF MENTORING

Learners, mentors and scheme organizers will be looking to the future to see the coming trends in mentoring, so that they can adapt these to their own needs and the needs of their organization.

The trends that we would like to highlight are the following:

☐ mentoring is becoming more central to development processes in organizations

☐ mentoring is different from other processes because of its emphasis on major transitions in the life of its participants

☐ mentoring is extending into forms other than the traditional one of a relationship between a junior individual and an off-line senior manager

☐ status issues are becoming less important in the mutual selection of mentors and learners

☐ there may be a contribution from mentoring to the erosion of traditional management prerogatives

☐ mentoring can grow best organically – out of the natural processes of affiliation and support that develop between people; and out of small pilot schemes run and sponsored by enthusiasts, which can grow and proliferate once their success has been demonstrated

☐ training for mentoring will increasingly develop away from a course-based strategy towards an approach which is more congruent with the mentoring process itself: networking as support for mentors or learners or both at once will become more widespread; shadow mentors – mentoring others who are developing in the role – will also be more widely used

☐ the learner will be seen as being at the centre of a network of relationships in which they engage for their own purposes, while being cognizant of the needs and urgencies of the organization.

The learner at the centre

Figure 1 showed a transition of responsibility for development from HRD to manager to mentor to learner. Figure 2 shows the development of this model, where the learner is at the centre, and calling upon a network of support for a variety of purposes.

This rich melange of resources is necessary in times where events and structures are unstable. A learner with a rich web of resources is hardly likely to lose them all at once. We have seen examples, in this book, of mentors carrying on supporting ex-employees, and we have experienced many instances of members of self-development groups continuing to attend even though they have left the organization. We came across one individual who in 18 months had three job moves and no less than seven bosses. The only point of stability in all this whirlwind of change was the relationship with a single mentor.

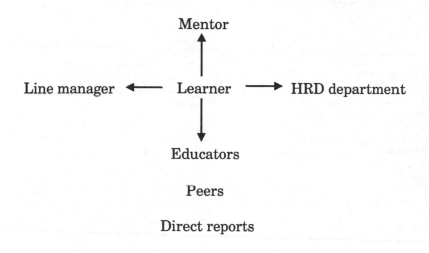

Figure 2 *Network of development with the learner at the centre*

INDEX